HOLY GHOST AND FIRE
HOLY GROUND

HOLY GHOST AND FIRE
HOLY GROUND

CARL L. WILSON, JR.

HOLY GHOST AND FIRE, HOLY GROUND

ISBN: 978-1-60402-884-3

Printed in the United States of America

© 2007 by Carl L. Wilson Jr.

1 2 3 4 5 6 7 8 9 10 / 12 11 10 09 08 07

CONTENTS

DEDICATION

This book is dedicated first to my wife, a true saint.
On many occasions I would say I felt led to work on the
book, and she would say, "I understand." She understands
the mission. She has a heart full of love and joy and
compassion for others. This book is also dedicated to my
sons, who gave up time with their dad. To all those who
teach and preach the truth of God's Word and not only what
people want to hear, and to all who take the time to read and
study the verses in this book. Also, I pray you feel the love
in which it is written. There is a hurting world out there! We
all need to stand shoulder to shoulder and be the light God
intended us to be with love, forgiveness, and power—
real power from God above.

PREFACE

I pray from the very beginning that this inspired book has achieved the goal before me, which is to clarify basic truths about the Christian faith. I thought many times so many others could have been chosen, but God chooses who He wants! As for serving God, the Lord Jesus Christ, it is not only a choice, it's a privilege. Each of us has an open-minded choice. The Christian faith is firmly built on three building blocks—God the Father, God the Son, and God the Holy Ghost! All three are alive and well, and though they are three, they are one, Jesus Christ being the chief cornerstone of the faith. This Godhead, as it is called, has not lost one ounce of its power. This faith is based on love, and genuine love for our fellow man. This includes love for their souls and the desire that everyone should be saved, that they would not perish into eternal damnation. And just for the record, this faith is not a cult or clique for only a chosen few! It is available to all. And I must add this: If someone is a full-blown alcoholic, drug addict, or sexual predator, wrapped in tremendous sin, are they labeled a fanatic by the world? Yet if a Christian is on fire for God, he is called a fanatic! Today the world seems to be a little mixed up, thinking bad is good and good is bad. This attitude is not of God.

HOLY GHOST AND FIRE, HOLY GROUND

In life we must strive to improve ourselves no matter what. With my own eyes I have seen many push to a higher calling in life. They have done so not only for worldly goods but to help others. Success is not only measured in possession of worldly goods. For a man can gain the whole world and lose his soul! God's Word states, *"I beseech you therefore, brethren, by the mercies of God, that ye present your bodies a living sacrifice, holy, acceptable unto God, which is your reasonable service. And be not conformed to this world: but be ye transformed by the renewing of your mind, that ye may prove what is that good, and acceptable, and perfect, will of God"* (Romans 12:1–2).

This press to improve oneself is a natural drive placed in all of us. As with government, military, and business, there are levels one can achieve through study and understanding. When it comes to spiritual achievement, it requires an opening of the mind to forces not always seen. Let's get on fire for God. *"I know thy works, that thou art neither cold nor hot: I would thou wert cold or hot. So then because thou art lukewarm, and neither cold nor hot, I will spue thee out of my mouth. Because thou sayest, I am rich, and increased with goods, and have need of nothing; and knowest not that thou art wretched, and miserable, and poor, and blind, and naked"* (Revelation 3:15–17).

Our Father in heaven did not give us life only to be destroyed. He wishes us to be fruitful and multiply. With power and grace, holy and acceptable to God!

This book is intended to shine a light on many subjects the enemy of our soul has tried to slide into the shadows. Today it seems many spend time and large sums of money trying to find any shred of evidence to disprove the truth. It also seems tomorrow's earth-shattering false claim is also the next big paycheck. The world continues to try to disprove the

Lord Jesus Christ! They deny the truth of His virgin birth, His life of love and miracles, His proclaiming of God's Word, His trial, His beating, His death and resurrection, and finally His translation into heaven. Deny all you want! I'm not one bit surprised. There are actually people today that deny the Holocaust ever happened. The Jewish people were born. They had families. Six million were tortured and murdered. The Germans kept records. We have survivors who fled the death camps. But still many don't believe.

If the world doubts what they can see, then why should they believe in a God they can't see! They still can see a glimpse of His power in people filled with the Holy Ghost! Miracles still take place every day! Let the world spend its millions in vain as they try to destroy the image of God and Jesus. Do you think that this generation is the first or last to come up against God? Let's look.

> *And when they had brought them, they set them before the council: and the high priest asked them, saying, Did not we straitly command you that ye should not teach in this name? and, behold, ye have filled Jerusalem with your doctrine, and intend to bring this man's blood upon us. Then Peter and the other apostles answered and said, We ought to obey God rather than men. The God of our fathers raised up Jesus, whom ye slew and hanged on a tree. Him hath God exalted with his right hand to be a Prince and a Saviour, for to give repentance to Israel, and forgiveness of sins. And we are his witnesses of these things; and so is also the Holy Ghost, whom God hath given to them that obey him.*
>
> (Acts 5:27–32)

Note: you might want to read verse 32 again!

HOLY GHOST AND FIRE, HOLY GROUND

Today it seems more and more ministries are straying farther and farther away from God's truth, His true holy Word, and power.

To those who deceive and twist the Word of God, I give you this verse. *"And then will I profess unto them, I never knew you: depart from me, ye that work iniquity"* (Matthew 7:23).

Attack the faith. It will stand! Attack God. He will stand!

My suggestion is that you open your Bible and verify the Scriptures in this book. I have used the King James Version of the Holy Bible. If you do not have a King James Version Bible, I will address that too.

God has winked at our ignorance long enough!

CHAPTER ONE

WHO IS THE HOLY GHOST?

H e is the one that always was and the one that always will be. *"Forasmuch then as we are the offspring of God, we ought not to think that the Godhead is like unto gold, or silver, or stone, graven by art and man's device"* (Acts 17:29).

The Holy Ghost is a mighty power source given by God the Father as a gift to believers. It is also sometimes referred to as the anointing. The anointing breaks off the yoke of bondage. The Holy Ghost is the doer of God's will. Depending on the situation, the anointing can be subdued or abound. Many today not only don't follow God's Word but they also believe the Holy Ghost was only given on the day of Pentecost and that the works of the apostles, such as miracles, healings, speaking in tongues etc., are a thing of the past!

We will review these claims and see how they line up with God's holy Word. There will be absolutely no guesswork. There was a police show when I was a child that my grandfather used to watch. When interviewing victims, the officer would state, "Just the facts ma'am. Just the facts." The Holy Ghost, the anointing, and His power are not anything to try to use for one's own advance. I would not have penned the first sentence if it were not called by God. There is a special joy in serving the Lord God. This joy is magnified when God commissions someone for a task. God commissions the authorization to perform certain duties or tasks or to take on certain power by giving such authority. God inspires at His will. Accept that He will use you. God gives authority and God takes away! Even this book may have critics come up against it. They will be judged accordingly. Not by man, but by God Himself. I too will be judged if I fail, but God will raise up another. He's God. He's never been defeated and never will!

CHAPTER TWO

WHY DO WE NEED THE HOLY GHOST?

From the first couple, Adam and Eve, until our present time, mankind has been under attack. Our attack comes from two sources. The first comes from ourselves. That's right. Many today try to blame others for their mistakes and shortcomings, but many times, it is our poorly made decisions that we make without any effort to seek God's guidance. We are basically telling God we don't need His advice or approval. Others throughout history thought they were above God's correction. They were sadly mistaken. Have you ever heard the famous quote about the Titanic? "Even God can't sink this ship!" It sank on its maiden voyage and now rusts on the bottom of the Atlantic Ocean. Let's take a valuable lesson from this. Let's not let our words or actions sink our future. God showed He loves us by sacrificing His only begotten Son, Jesus Christ. God will not tolerate our disobedience or mocking Him at any level. Don't sink your own ship.

Would you like to tap into God's endless wisdom and knowledge? Why do so many try to take everything on themselves? You don't have to. He's always there, twenty-four hours a day! Seek His help.

Second, we have an enemy who has tried to destroy mankind from the first couple. This unseen enemy twists and turns, working evil every day. With the skill of a spider, he builds a web for his victims. This enemy is a powerful fallen angel cast down from heaven for disobedience and rebellion. His name, Satan, means adversary. He is also called Abaddon and Appolyon, the destroyer. You can see his work by the level of depravity and evil that man puts toward his fellow man! Though given power from God, Satan is not all-powerful, but he does have power! Some have spoken and called him a toothless lion. If he's toothless, then there should be no more rapes, murders, shootings, kidnappings, or robberies! Shall I go on?

Do you think we live in a peaceful world? Let's take a look at Satan's very nature.

> *Ye are of your father the devil, and the lusts of your father ye will do. He was a murderer from the beginning, and abode not in the truth, because there is no truth in him. When he speaketh a lie, he speaketh of his own: for he is a liar, and the father of it.* (John 8:44)

This powerful angel even tried to tempt Jesus.

> *Then was Jesus led up of the Spirit into the wilderness to be tempted of the devil. And when he had fasted forty days and forty nights, he was afterward an hungered. And when the tempter came to him, he said, If thou be the Son of God, command that these stones be made bread. But he answered and said, It is written, Man shall not live by bread alone, but by every word that proceedeth out of the mouth of God.*

Why Do We Need the Holy Ghost?

Then the devil taketh him up into the holy city, and setteth him on a pinnacle of the temple, and saith unto him, If thou be the Son of God, cast thyself down: for it is written, He shall give his angels charge concerning thee: and in their hands they shall bear thee up, lest at any time thou dash thy foot against a stone. Jesus said unto him, It is written again, Thou shalt not tempt the Lord thy God. Again, the devil taketh him up into an exceeding high mountain, and showeth him all the kingdoms of the world, and the glory of them; and saith unto him, All these things will I give thee, if thou wilt fall down and worship me. Then saith Jesus unto him, Get thee hence, Satan: for it is written, Thou shalt worship the Lord thy God, and him only shalt thou serve. Then the devil leaveth him, and, behold, angels came and ministered unto him. (Matthew 4:1–11)

The devil had enough nerve to stand and tempt Jesus Christ. How do you think you will stand when trials or tests come? Will you stand or buckle, like so many? For Satan seeks every soul he can steal or those that are handed to him. For when the end has come and God casts Satan into the pits of hell to burn forever, he wants company! Every soul he claims for evil is a trophy he can show to God. As he collects souls daily, he must laugh at our weakness and stupidity.

Weak from a Lack of Power

The question again is why do we need the power of the Holy Ghost?

In Acts 19:11–12, we find in the apostle Paul performing miracles and casting out demons. Demons are evil spirits, eternal beings. When God flooded the earth in Noah's time, where did all the demons go? Or where did all the demons from

15

Sodom and Gomorrah go? Simple. They're still here! If you don't think so, watch the news! Pure evil is being unleashed daily all over the world!

Let's take a look at what happens when well-wishers try to take matters into their own hands without the Holy Ghost!

> *Then certain of the vagabond Jews, exorcists, took upon them to call over them which had evil spirits the name of the Lord Jesus, saying, We adjure you by Jesus whom Paul preacheth. And there were seven sons of one Sceva, a Jew, and chief of the priests, which did so. And the evil spirit answered and said, Jesus I know, and Paul I know; but who are ye? And the man in whom the evil spirit was leaped on them, and overcame them, and prevailed against them, so that they fled out of that house naked and wounded.*
>
> (Acts 19:13-17)

First they took it upon themselves to cast out demons. They were not sent by God, even though they used Jesus' name! They were not saved, sanctified, or Holy Ghost filled. The evil spirit said, "I don't know you!" He jumped them and beat them. Our spiritual life is not a joke! Some will say we are too serious. Think on this. How many times have you heard someone speaking about hell like it's an amusement park? Let me remind all, God our Father implanted super-sensitive nerve endings throughout our body for pleasure. This same God who invented pleasure has created the very pits of hell. Hell is an eternal torture chamber where death would be a relief. Will the inhabitants also see people they knew in the vilest of possible places forever and ever and ever?

16

Why Do We Need the Holy Ghost?

Why do we need the Holy Ghost? We are in a battle for our very souls, not to mention the potential of billions lost.

We need all of God's power we can get!

Principles!

That's what we need!

I was sitting by an evangelist after he had preached a sermon. We were just chatting about the Bible. Then he wanted to debate the Bible, which I will not do! God is love. His Word should not make us argue. There are some issues that should be so clear there should be no debate! One morning, my wife told me there was a certain Bible teacher on TV. I like his lessons, but when he sees "the Holy Ghost" in the Bible he says, "the Holy Spirit!" When I hear these types of things, it's a true test of my sanctification. For as Jesus threw the money changers out of the temple, I get very upset at anyone who alters the Word of God for their personal gain. I don't care whether their title is bishop, doctor, overseer, pastor, or deacon. It makes me want to rend my clothes. Don't people have enough to fight about without someone spinning the Word of God? Who are they trying to impress?

I'm burning up! I have a great deal of respect for firemen, doctors, caregivers, and emergency responders on any level where the loss of human life is possible. One mistake, and a life is lost. Our burden is not completely different. If I fail the mission before me, those souls I was destined to teach and preach the Word of God to are lost. Their blood is on my hands! And their souls will burn for an eternity!

Back to the point. Why do educated men and women of faith say what is not in the Bible? Could they think they are smarter than God? We need a new style of religion. Why? Let's look at another example.

SHOW ME THE WORD RAPTURE

It's not in the Bible. Then why preach it?

Here let me show you what it says.

*By faith Enoch was translated that he should not see death; and was not found, because God had translated him: **for before** his translation he had this testimony, that he pleased God.* (Hebrew 11:5)

The subject of pleasing God could fill another book! But let's look at what this verse says. Did the Bible say "rapture," did it say he went up in a hot air balloon or a big soap bubble?

No, it says that Enoch was "translated." Do you understand the danger of changing words in the Bible?

Perhaps you say, "Oh, minister, you are overreacting!" Am I? Have you over been on a farm? They say, "If you see one mouse or rat there are usually more!" Well, I smell more than a rat. I smell a trap set by Satan himself to deceive all Christians! He wants to take away our power to stand and fight!

I looked up the word *translate* in the dictionary. For the record, since most of us don't speak Greek or Hebrew, King James and others graciously had the Bible translated for us.

Translate is defined as:

1) To move from one place or condition to another, transfer: Theology to convey directly to heaven without death.

2) To transfer (a bishop) from one see to another; also to move (a saint's body or remains) from one place of interest to another.

3) To change into another medium or translate ideas into action.

4) To put into different words rephrase or paraphrase in explanation.

5) To transmit (a telegraph message) again by means of an automatic relay.

6) Archaic to entrap: to entrance

7) To impart translation into another language, to be capable of being translated

Translation also means a "motion in which every point of the moving object has simultaneously the same velocity and direction of motion."

There is more, but that's enough! Now translation implies there is one who translates. Who or what would have the power to translate a human?

When God the Father sends Jesus back for the saints to bring us home, will we be ready? You've got it. We will be translated home! Even the ones in the tombs will rise. Some may not believe that either. It has happened in the past.

I don't know about you, but as for me, when the great Translator wants to translate me, I want to be prayed up and translated up!

I'm sure some probably won't believe that is going to happen. But the Bible repeats itself.

Jesus, when he had cried again with a loud voice, yielded up the ghost. And, behold, the veil of the temple was rent in twain from the top to the bottom; and the earth did quake, and the rocks rent; and the graves were opened; and many

bodies of the saints which slept arose, and came out of the graves after his resurrection, and went into the holy city, and appeared unto many. (Matthew 27:50–53)

The dead shall rise and be translated! It's in the Bible!

Let's answer the question, Why do we need the Holy Ghost?

First, to withstand the direct attacks of demonic powers and to have supernatural help in pushing away from sin.

There is also a second answer. Please take time to understand this revelation. As a child, I remember my grandparents stressing the importance of school, college, and buying a house. When the house is paid off, you are more secure, and you can pay off other bills with the money you were using on the mortgage. The result is financial freedom! Then there is, in most cases, an inheritance. You leave a legacy of your hard work, a mind-set that you want your children to have it better than you did. It is a blessing to have an inheritance left to our children and our children's children.

Now, look at the world. What does everyone seek besides love? Comfort! Today, so many are seeking to fit in that they go to extreme measures like plastic surgery. Why? They need comfort that they look good. Why do so many work hard to reach their retirement goals? Comfort! From early cave dwellers to this very day, the human race seeks, strives, and desires one thing—comfort!

Before Jesus ascended to heaven, He spoke, "My Father will send another Comforter. This Comforter will not only live with you, but in you!" This gift is from God. He has offered the ultimate Comforter. The power given on Pentecost is available to this very day.

Jesus and God have given us part of our heavenly inheritance before we are taken home in glory. Please grab this part!

When a loved one dies, some families retain lawyers and fight over the family's inheritance. In many cases, hatred arises, and when it's divided, it weakens, as each gets their portion. But, brothers and sisters, as this inheritance is divided, it gains in power! As you will find, when those gather that are filled, the anointing increases. The ultimate inheritance and the ultimate comforter! So let's rejoice and receive our promised inheritance.

The ultimate Comforter is the Holy Ghost. It's our inheritance.

CHAPTER THREE

WHY DO WE NEED TO STAND?

First and foremost, we need to take a stand for ourselves! On judgment day, there will be no one to point a finger at and say, "He or she made me do it." At the end of our mortal life, there is a judgment! When we are born, our eternal life has begun. Eternal life is not a choice, but where we spend it is. Yes, being saved is important, but we will all be judged. Even me, for I'm no better than anyone. Let's look at the judgment.

> *And I saw a great white throne, and him that sat on it, from whose face the earth and the heaven fled away; and there was found no place for them. And I saw the dead, small and great, stand before God; and the books were opened: and another book was opened, which is the book of life: and the dead were judged out of those things which were written in the books, according to their works. And the sea gave up the dead which were in it; and death and hell delivered up the dead which were in them: and they were judged every man according to their works. And death and hell were cast into the lake of fire. This is the second death. And whosoever was*

not found written in the book of life was cast into the lake of
fire.   (Revelation 20:11–15)

Are you written in the Lamb's book of life? Have you been saved, truly saved?

Jesus came for many missions, but His greatest was to free man from sin. Each of us can now be cleansed of sin. We must be reborn! This is done in a two-part process. First, we must believe that Jesus Christ is God's Son who died for our sins. Second, we must understand all have sinned, and come up short. We must repent and ask God to forgive us of our sins in His Son's name. We must state this out loud. We must ask Jesus to come into our hearts and make us new. This is being saved. Your past sins are thrown into the sea of forgetfulness.

We must also understand that when Jesus died, He was buried, then resurrected, and then ascended to heaven and sits at the right hand of the Father. These basic revelations are the beginning of the Christian faith walk.

If you are at this point, you are now saved, so speak it and live it! You are just at the beginning!

Some will say, "Minister, I've heard this before! That's great, but not everyone who reads this book may be a Christian or already saved." Did you ever play a sport? Professional athletes practice the basics over and over again until they become the best at the game. You must go over the basics no matter how advanced your walk.

Words are powerful. As Christians, we are called to speak things as they will be. For the longest time I had a sticky note on my bathroom mirror. It said, "I'm blessed, I'm anointed, and I'm highly favored." Speak it like it will be!

The Christian faith is a faith of faith! A faith where we give as God gave His only begotten Son for us. When we receive the gift of salvation, we want to give to others. And we have a desire to give back to God! Salvation is not something we can earn. It is a gift from God, paid for by Jesus Christ at a price we could never pay, to be free from hell and eternal damnation!

What if God had never sent Jesus! But He did! But at what cost, a death horrible more than the human mind can comprehend. This is well documented. What if salvation had a price? What if instead of repenting and asking God to forgive us in Jesus' name of our sins, He wanted more to set us free from hell's chains of torture? What if He demanded your sight for the rest of your life or the use of a limb? Possibly a sickness or loss of hearing. If you knew what hell was like, you would willingly give up these things and much more in order ot avoid it! Thank God, He requires none of these! As I write, I can only imagine the ones who read my books saying how do all these things fit together? Well, if I were writing books for my own benefit, I could see their point. But the books I write are inspired.

I was preaching to a group of ministers. At the time I was questioning my qualifications. As I brought the Word of God, we were in a park and runners and joggers were passing us. I said, "Do you see how hard they work on the body, which is non-eternal and will eventually die? But what about the inside—the eternal. How real is life, and how final is death! To the body, death is the end, but to the soul, it is the beginning." Eternal life is not a choice. Where we spend it is. To God be the glory.

As we fight this battle, it comes from many sides. The internal conflict is the first obstacle. We seem to have a built-in self-destructive nature, a tendency to look at things negatively. If I took a piece of white copy paper, placed a black dot about the size of a dime in the center, then asked one million people, "What do you see?" most would say, "A black spot." How many do you think would even mention the paper? We need to get the whole picture! Many questions may always be there. Why was I born? What is my destiny? What am I supposed to do? What do I believe? Do I have my own sense of what is right or am I being influenced by the world to tell me what's right? Do I pretend something is right when deep in my very soul I know it's wrong? My brothers and sisters, you must make the difference. We can't wait for someone else. It may be too late for you and countless others. Learn from Christ's example: one person can change the world for right! You be that person! Someone must lead. You be that person. You are important to God. You are loved.

I must add this important paragraph. Where did all these types of churches come from? Why do we have so many denominations? What do they stand for? Do they even know?

The word *denomination* comes from *denominate*, which means "to name."

Denomination also means "a class or kind of units in a system having a specific name or value."

So it is a division into units. Now, who is the father of division? That's right—Satan!

He wants to split Christians into as many groups as possible. He wants to have these groups interpret the Bible as differently as possible to stir up uncooperation and even dislike for branches that believe differently.

His strategy can be summed up as divide and conquer!

Holy Ghost and Fire, Holy Ground

A divided Christianity leads to weak Christianity. When was the last time your church had a fellowship with another branch of faith? It matters! We will be judged on how we treat all!

> *Then they that feared the LORD spake often one to another: and the LORD hearkened, and heard it, and a book of remembrance was written before him for them that feared the LORD, and that thought upon his name.* (Malachi 3:16)

When they open the books, how will you stand?

I say with all the love that is in me, we are in a battle. It's multisided. We must fight for ourselves, our family, and all the others we touch. I don't want the blood of the souls I was to win on my hands!

We will not be able postpone our final judgment. So be prepared. Don't wait until later. Later always comes, and often catches one unprepared!

CHAPTER FOUR

WHO HAD THE HOLY GHOST IN THE BIBLE?

Many in the Bible received the gift of the indwelling of the Holy Ghost. Some today claim it was only given on the day of Pentecost and ceased to operate. Let's review the Scriptures and see with our own eyes.

> *And when they agreed not among themselves, they departed, after that Paul had spoken one word, Well spake the Holy Ghost by Esaias [Isaiah] the prophet unto our fathers.*
>
> (Acts 28:25)

One sign that one has the Holy Ghost is when he speaks through an individual. Isaiah had the Holy Ghost.

David is one of my favorite leaders in the Bible. He was a man of courage and strength, who could praise God from deep in his soul. His inspired words have comforted me many times. I also have heard it taught he did not have the Holy Ghost! *"For David himself said by the Holy Ghost, The LORD said to my Lord, Sit thou on my right hand, till I make thine enemies thy footstool"* (Mark 12:36). Imagine my surprise when I looked upon this verse!

David said it *"by the Holy Ghost"*! David had an indwelling of the Holy Ghost!

Also, in Psalm 39:2–3, we read,

I was dumb with silence, I held my peace, even from good; and my sorrow was stirred. My heart was hot within me, while I was musing the fire burned: then spake I with my tongue.

The Bible says David had the Holy Ghost, and are these verses a reference to speaking in tongues? If it's not, what was he using before?

Fact: David had the Holy Ghost!

The New Testament also has many examples for us to study. First is John the Baptist's mother, Elizabeth.

And it came to pass, that, when Elisabeth heard the saluta-tion of Mary, the babe leaped in her womb; and Elisabeth was filled with the Holy Ghost.   (Luke 1:41)

Elizabeth had the Holy Ghost!

What about John the Baptist's father, Zachariah? Did he have it?

There was in the days of Herod, the king of Judaea, a certain priest named Zacharias, of the course of Abia: and his wife was of the daughters of Aaron, and her name was Elisabeth. And they were both righteous before God, walking in all the commandments and ordinances of the Lord blameless. And they had no child, because that Elisabeth was barren, and they both were now well stricken in years. And it came to pass, that while he executed the priest's office before God in the order of his course, according to the custom of the priest's office, his lot was to burn incense when he went into the temple of the Lord. And the whole multitude of the people were praying without at the time of incense. And there appeared unto him an angel of the Lord standing on the right side of the altar of incense. And when Zacharias saw him, he was troubled, and fear fell upon him. But the angel said unto him, Fear not, Zacharias: for thy prayer is heard; and thy wife Elisabeth shall bear thee a son, and thou shalt call his name John. And thou shalt have joy and gladness; and many shall rejoice at his birth. (Luke 1:5–14)

Question: Who was the first to receive the Holy Ghost? John the Baptist, his mother, Elizabeth, or his father, Zachariah?

Look at the next verse:

For he shall be great in the sight of the Lord, and shall drink neither wine nor strong drink; and he shall be filled with the Holy Ghost, even from his mother's womb. (Luke 1:15)

John the Baptist had the Holy Ghost!

THE ANGEL OF THE LORD

And the angel answering said unto him, I am Gabriel, that stand in the presence of God; and am sent to speak unto thee, and to show thee these glad tidings. And, behold, thou shalt be dumb, and not able to speak, until the day that these things shall be performed, because thou believest not my words, which shall be fulfilled in their season. And the people waited for Zacharias, and marvelled that he tarried so long in the temple. And when he came out, he

29

could not speak unto them: and they perceived that he had seen a vision in the temple: for he beckoned unto them, and remained speechless. And it came to pass, that, as soon as the days of his ministration were accomplished, he departed to his own house. And after those days his wife Elisabeth conceived, and hid herself five months, saying, Thus hath the Lord dealt with me in the days wherein he looked on me, to take away my reproach among men.   (Luke 1:19–25)

THE BIRTH OF JOHN THE BAPTIST

Now Elisabeth's full time came that she should be delivered; and she brought forth a son. And her neighbours and her cousins heard how the Lord had showed great mercy upon her; and they rejoiced with her. And it came to pass, that on the eighth day they came to circumcise the child; and they called him Zacharias, after the name of his father. And his mother answered and said, Not so; but he shall be called John. And they said unto her, There is none of thy kindred that is called by this name. And they made signs to his father, how he would have him called. And he asked for a writing table, and wrote, saying, His name is John. And they marvelled all. And his mouth was opened immediately, and his tongue loosed, and he spake, and praised God. And fear came on all that dwelt round about them: and all these sayings were noised abroad throughout all the hill country of Judaea. And all they that heard them laid them up in their hearts, saying, What manner of child shall this be! And the hand of the Lord was with him. And his father Zacharias was filled with the Holy Ghost, and prophesied, saying, Blessed be the Lord God of Israel; for he hath visited and redeemed his people, and hath raised up an horn of salvation for us in the house of his servant David; as he spake by the mouth of his holy prophets, which have been since the world began: that we should be saved from our enemies, and from the hand of all that hate us; to perform the mercy promised to our fathers, and to remember his holy covenant.

(Luke 1:57–72)

Zechariah was filled with the Holy Ghost!

So Elizabeth (the mother), then John the Baptist, then Zechariah (the father)—they all had the Holy Ghost! What a family!

The Big Question is: Did Jesus, the cornerstone of the faith, have the Holy Ghost?

And in the sixth month the angel Gabriel was sent from God unto a city of Galilee, named Nazareth, to a virgin espoused to a man whose name was Joseph, of the house of David; and the virgin's name was Mary. And the angel came in unto her, and said, Hail, thou that art highly favoured, the Lord is with thee: blessed art thou among women. And when she saw him, she was troubled at his saying, and cast in her mind what manner of salutation this should be. And the angel said unto her, Fear not, Mary: for thou hast found favour with God. And, behold, thou shalt conceive in thy womb, and bring forth a son, and shalt call his name Jesus. He shall be great, and shall be called the Son of the Highest: and the Lord God shall give unto him the throne of his father David: and he shall reign over the house of Jacob for ever; and of his kingdom there shall be no end. Then said Mary unto the angel, How shall this be, seeing I know not a man? And the angel answered and said unto her, The Holy Ghost shall come upon thee, and the power of the Highest shall overshadow thee: therefore also that holy thing which shall be born of thee shall be called the Son of God. And, behold, thy cousin Elisabeth, she hath also conceived a son in her old age: and this is the sixth month with her, who was called barren. For with God nothing shall be impossible. And Mary said, Behold the handmaid of the Lord; be it unto me according to thy word. And the angel departed from her.

(Luke 1:26–38)

So let's get this right! If the Holy Ghost had not overshadowed Mary, there would have been no Jesus Christ of Nazareth!

This leaves a large question. Did Jesus receive the indwelling of the Holy Ghost and when? Let's look.

These things were done in Bethabara beyond Jordan, where John was baptizing. The next day John seeth Jesus coming unto him, and saith, Behold the Lamb of God, which taketh away the sin of the world. This is he of whom I said, After me cometh a man which is preferred before me: for he was before me. And I knew him not: but that he should be made manifest to Israel, therefore am I come baptizing with water. And John bare record, saying, I saw the Spirit descending from heaven like a dove, and it abode upon him. And I knew him not: but he that sent me to baptize with water, the same said unto me, Upon whom thou shalt see the Spirit descending, and remaining on him, the same is he which baptizeth with the Holy Ghost. And I saw, and bare record that this is the Son of God.

(John 1:28–34)

John said Jesus received the Holy Ghost and received it as the second baptism from God!

Jesus also baptized with the Holy Ghost!

WHO HAD THE HOLY GHOST IN THE BIBLE?

John answered, saying unto them all, I indeed baptize you with water; but one mightier than I cometh, the latchet of whose shoes I am not worthy to unloose: he shall baptize you with the Holy Ghost and with fire....Now when all the people were baptized, it came to pass, that Jesus also being baptized, and praying, the heaven was opened, and the Holy Ghost descended in a bodily shape like a dove upon him, and a voice came from heaven, which said, Thou art my beloved Son; in thee I am well pleased. (Luke 3:16, 21–22)

Jesus received the full indwelling, after He was first baptized for the remission of sins, though He was sin free. Why would He do this? He did this because He was fully human, yet perfect. He did it to give us an example that even He should be humble before a mighty God. The Holy Ghost descended and the anointing stayed! Jesus had the Holy Ghost!

Some will ask did Jesus received the Holy Ghost at birth? No! His first miracle happened *after* receiving the Holy Ghost when He turned water into wine. And why would He need to receive it again if He had it already?

When Jesus was born, He was taken to the high priest, Simeon, to be consecrated, a Jewish custom.

And, behold, there was a man in Jerusalem, whose name was Simeon; and the same man was just and devout, waiting for the consolation of Israel: and the Holy Ghost was upon him. And it was revealed unto him by the Holy Ghost, that he should not see death, before he had seen the Lord's Christ. (Luke 2:25–26)

Simeon had the Holy Ghost.

What about the disciples?

33

Jesus had given them power, in John 20:19–23.

Then the same day at evening, being the first day of the week, when the doors were shut where the disciples were assembled for fear of the Jews, came Jesus and stood in the midst, and saith unto them, Peace be unto you. And when he had so said, he showed unto them his hands and his side. Then were the disciples glad, when they saw the Lord. Then said Jesus to them again, Peace be unto you: as my Father hath sent me, even so send I you. And when he had said this, he breathed on them, and saith unto them, Receive ye the Holy Ghost: Whose soever sins ye remit, they are remitted unto them; and whose soever sins ye retain, they are retained.

So all the disciples, except Doubting Thomas, who was not there that day, were filled. Is that why so many lack today?

And when they were come in, they went up into an upper room, where abode both Peter, and James, and John, and Andrew, Philip, and Thomas, Bartholomew, and Matthew, James the son of Alphaeus, and Simon Zelotes, and Judas the brother of James. These all continued with one accord in prayer and supplication, with the women, and Mary the mother of Jesus, and with his brethren. (Acts 1:13–14)

And when the day of Pentecost was fully come, they were all with one accord in one place. And suddenly there came a sound from heaven as of a rushing mighty wind, and it filled all the house where they were sitting. And there appeared unto them cloven tongues like as of fire, and it sat upon each of them. And they were all filled with the Holy Ghost, and began to speak with other tongues, as the Spirit gave them utterance. (Acts 2:1–4)

Who Had the Holy Ghost in the Bible?

This Jesus hath God raised up, whereof we all are witnesses. Therefore being by the right hand of God exalted, and having received of the Father the promise of the Holy Ghost, he hath shed forth this, which ye now see and hear. For David is not ascended into the heavens: but he saith himself, The Lord said unto my Lord, Sit thou on my right hand, until I make thy foes thy footstool. Therefore let all the house of Israel know assuredly, that God hath made that same Jesus, whom ye have crucified, both Lord and Christ. Now when they heard this, they were pricked in their heart, and said unto Peter and to the rest of the apostles, Men and brethren, what shall we do? Then Peter said unto them, Repent, and be baptized every one of you in the name of Jesus Christ for the remission of sins, and ye shall receive the gift of the Holy Ghost. For the promise is unto you, and to your children, and to all that are afar off, even as many as the Lord our God shall call. And with many other words did he testify and exhort, saying, Save yourselves from this untoward generation. Then they that gladly received his word were baptized: and the same day there were added unto them about three thousand souls. And they continued stedfastly in the apostles' doctrine and fellowship, and in breaking of bread, and in prayers. (Acts 2:32–42)

Take another look at verse 39! *"For the promise is unto you, and to your children, and to all that are afar off, even as many as the Lord our God shall call."*

The promise has not changed! Only the lack of commitment and resolve of the saints has changed! If you believe it, you can receive it!

CHAPTER FIVE

THE VOICE

I t came so softly throughout my life, at different times. My inner self had feelings, such as, stay, go, be careful, or you should not be here. But this was different. As a small child, I had attended a Christian preschool. I remember a large Gothic church with large stone walls and a large playground. I remember a feeling of being safe there. As I grew older, I attended a Lutheran church, primarily for Sunday school. An incident happened when I was nine. My parents had asked the pastor if he would baptize my new baby brother. He declined because my parents were not members. This was very upsetting since my little brother was born with heart problems. At that point, we stopped attending church altogether.

Years passed, and my neighbor, who was a Sunday school teacher in a large Methodist church, must have talked to my parents about taking me on Sundays. This man drove me year after year. How he ever put up with my know-it-all attitude must have been the love of Christ. I recently called to thank him and inform him he did not waste his time! As I grew older, in my late teens, I stopped attending again. Part of my unplanned escape was to work Sundays. Satan fully cooperated. Through all my antics, God kept His hand on me.

After completing high school, my means of transportation was a small motorcycle. Boy, I thought I was something. I rode year-round, wet roads, icy roads, snow, and sleet. I even remember my jeans freezing stiff from freezing rain. One night, my carefree attitude caught up with me. Riding with friends on a cold winter night, we were going over a bridge. Thank God that no traffic was coming. The bridge was icy. I apparently hit an icy spot, lost control, and slid on my back twenty or thirty feet. I was okay, but when my helmet touched the road, I could hear the grinding of the pavement passing the protective shell into the foam! I did not even receive a scratch! If I had fallen face first, I would hate to think what I may look like now!

I will spare you some of the following years, but they were full of casual drunkenness, disrespect, disposable relationships, and ignorance that I showed to many. My friends were assisting in my decline, but I was a willing vessel.

However, God will send a breakthrough from unlikely places. A coworker and friend approached me one fall afternoon. When you work outside year-round in Maryland, in the fall, winter crosses your mind! He said, "Here, look at these photos." They were from the Florida Keys. He said, "Man, do you see this?" He had just returned from working on a shrimp boat. With the Gulf's blue waters, fishing, eating shrimp, making great money. He told me, "Man, these guys, when they hit big shrimp, they could make a thousand dollars a day!" At the time, I was working two jobs just to survive and making about three hundred dollars a week! With winter coming, what was I waiting for? So we were off to Marathon

Key to go on vacation and get rich on one of those beautiful luxury shrimp hotel boats! I was sure there was a waiting list. I figured it might be a few weeks before I could get on one. But these kinds of thoughts are only minor details when you are on a mission!

There were only a few tiny details my friend forgot to point out. For example, you have to start at the bottom. First, there is not any paperwork required. If you fell overboard, they don't even know your full name. Second, there are not any special requirements. We would not be on the same ship—no big deal. The thought you could be working with anyone wasn't the most comforting. To find a job, we went from boat to boat and asked if they needed help. I cannot write their complete response. It usually consisted of, "Look, where are you from? If you were smart, you should get in your truck and head home," and enough curse words to make a sailor blush. But they didn't understand that I was on a mission.

I found a job on a boat that was quite a gem. On the first night out of port, we almost sank. The bilge pumps were failing. Cowboy, the first mate, told me to go to the deck, lean over, and see if any water was coming out! It was rough, so I leaned over to look holding on for dear life. At that point, all joking was over. I was in a real man's situation. And if I goofed around, I would be shark bait! There were a few other tiny details my friend had forgotten to mention. For instance, the second mate slept in the lower bunk directly above the engine room. It did have a two-inch piece of foam. It was like sleeping in a sauna. Then there are absolutely no bathroom facilities. All personal business was conducted over the rail. No shower. Well, I'll tell you, after having jelly fish and all kinds of slime fall on me all night—yes, we shrimped all night!—I could not stand it. I had to use some of my water ration to wash off. At this point, you are thinking, what in the world does this have to do with the Holy Ghost? You'll see!

I had heard the expression, "That's the way it goes. First your money, then your clothes!" They were right. My high-paying shrimping carrier was not paying off too good in cash! The salt water was destroying my clothes. They were also right that the captains who hit big shrimp made big money! The captains I had seemed to hit every wreck in the Gulf! Lose your rig, go home broke! One time I did make one hundred twenty three dollars. For two weeks out in the Gulf in storms.

If that sounds tough, years earlier the captain was caught illegally shrimping off French Guinea and put in jail where he acquired the taste for hot food. I mean hot! A bologna sandwich was a delicacy, but I was not a quitter. God had a purpose. Out to sea, there was no TV, no alcohol, and no friends to influence me. I was getting reprogrammed. I had thoughts, *I could do better than this. God does not want Christians to quit or give up! We as Christians should expect to move up. Be ready for it.* I had more than a sense that this was not where I belonged!

After a few more months of going out weeks on end and being in storms so big they almost flipped the boat over, I remember two specific incidents. In the first one, we were anchored, and the captain was showing us how to repair nets. These huge waves, I would say fifteen or twenty feet, were going under us. It was like being on an elevator. Up and down, up and down! The second more serious incident, we were bringing in our nets. A storm was tossing us. Where we pushed the debris out, as the boat turned, a wave hit the hole and shot a cannon of water right at me, almost blowing me over the side. If Terry, the first mate, had not grabbed me, no one would have heard me yell over the wind and engine noise! He grabbed me just before I went over! This was dangerous. For example, our wooden lifeboat was nailed to the top of the ship. It was no help!

I had a small journal. I remember writing, "God, please help me! God, I will take any selling job You can give me." Remembering my past, I thought, *When I was a salesman, I was happier talking with people.* God answered my prayer. I wrote a letter to my aunt and uncle, and a kind Christian family let me stay with them a while. I was not the best houseguest. After about a year and a half, I traveled back to Maryland. Years followed, and many events unfolded. But God was about to give me one of my greatest gifts, my wife Christine. Along with my new wife came her family, a family rooted in God, with a strong Pentecostal faith. One Sunday after the service, the pastor asked, "Did you like it?" I said I was used to unleaded, and this was definitely high-test.

My new brothers-in-law wasted no time informing me that all that cursing I was doing was not necessary, was offensive, and I was better than that. They were right. As time passed and with more visits, the convicting power of the Holy Ghost started to work on me.

We had heard many times about an anointed pastor. He was going to be in a nearby town the next weekend. It was as if a homing beacon was set off within me. A driving force was almost pulling me to North Carolina. This would be a weekend trip. Six hours each way and, with food, gas, tolls, and a possible trip to the mall, it could get a little expensive. Nothing was going to stop me! The revival was awesome. As the evening drew toward an end, he called, "Does anyone here want a closer walk with the Lord?" Nothing was going to stop me! I must have almost run to the altar. As he came up to me and leaned forward, I said in his ear, "I have known of Jesus but I want to know Him better." He stepped back, and he looked up a second or two. He said, "Him, Lord!" A big smile came upon his face. He said, "I don't know what it is, but the Lord has big plans for you!" He placed his hands on my face, one on each side. A powerful electric shock shot through me. I had in the past said a sinner's prayer. But this was different. It was the power of the Holy Ghost. I could not talk. My tongue rolled around in my head. I think it was minutes before I could speak. God had done a work in me that flooded my soul. I may have spoken that I was saved many times, but this anointing changed me forever!

I remember a television evangelist on very late night; he used to say place your hand on the screen. Repeat after me. But that was fifteen years ago. This was different! I was not saved by the laying on of hands. But whatever was hindering me was broken off by the Holy Ghost's miracle working power. On the way home, all I could do was sing "He Touched Me." As time progressed, my mother in law told me to find a local church, a Holy Ghost filled church. One that teaches out of the King James Bible. Was she ever right!

As I sit in traffic or a gust of diesel smoke comes my way, it reminds me of so many lonely nights on the back of a shrimp boat, sitting on a little wooden seat culling and sorting through tons of fish, crabs, and all kinds of unusual looking things from the bottom of the Gulf. We sat there hour after hour, with that smoke blowing in our faces. It's still in my memory bank along with the fact that a loving God pulled me from the path of destruction and turned me around and planted my feet on solid ground, the Lord Jesus Christ!

Chapter Six

The Light

We moved to the farm country of the Eastern shore of Maryland. Some call it the land of pleasant living. With the ocean on one side and the Chesapeake Bay on the other, we were surrounded by spectacular views, wildlife, and seafood. It's a wonderful place to raise a family. We were blessed to find a house, which my wife converted into a beautiful home. We had been blessed with a new child just a few weeks earlier. A few weeks after we moved in, my boss called. He wanted to meet at 10 am Friday at the same location where I was hired. In the meeting, he informed me the company would no longer desire my services. I was in shock. I had a new baby and a new house, and I had not saved any money for emergencies. He had given little indication he was unhappy with my progress. I found out later the company was pulling out of the area and was soon to be sold. The next weekend, we had plans to visit a large amusement park. I informed my brother-in-law, who lives life as a Christian, of the situation. He's not a talker, and his response was, "Can I help?" We went home with a sense that someone would help.

Being saved at the time. I would praise God, sing, and rejoice. But now my singing had turned to sorrow. I had cried out to God many times. "God, please help me! I need You, God. I'm forty years old. I know You did not bring me this far to fail now!" Driving home one afternoon after a few days of grey skies, the sky was dark grey from horizon to horizon. I was taking a back road home. All of a sudden the sky opened up right over me. A bright ray of sunlight shone directly on the vehicle through the windshield, and right on me! I almost immediately stopped crying, and I felt a peace come over me that everything would be all right. I had received comfort.

A day or so later, I was taking a shower. A voice spoke a verse out of the Bible into my spirit. It was not like someone talking with their mouth. This voice was right inside me! It was like a thought. The voice said Deuteronomy 8, verse 4. I finished my shower and thought no more about it. A little later as I was dressing, I mentioned it to my wife. Not knowing the Bible very well, at the time it didn't mean much to me. A few hours later, I finally opened my Bible. I was floored, I mean shocked! *"Thy raiment waxed not old upon thee, neither did thy foot swell, these forty years."* God had answered my prayers! What did I have to fear? God had told me in His Word, "I have taken care of you so far. Why do you doubt Me now?" This changed my life. God's help came quick and strong. At a later date, God blessed me with a job that paid double.

CHAPTER SEVEN

SAVED, THEN SANCTIFIED

You must be saved, then sanctified, then filled with the Holy Ghost—unless God does all three at once! I heard that preached for seven or more years. You may not agree. At first neither did I. But if you open your mind to the truth of God's Word, He will enlighten you if you let Him. Maybe you've never heard anyone else teach this. If you want to be like the rest of the world, you will be denying the blessings of God. It's simple: choose this day whom you will serve!

When I was newly saved, I started to read the Bible more and more. It is full of awesome stories and very strong words. I asked my wife in private, "Are you sure all these things in the Bible actually happened? Is what we are hearing preached true? I mean is this all real?"

When we went to church that Sunday, boy oh boy was I going to get my answer! Our pastor's wife was teaching Sunday school. This little lady was a powerful teacher. As she was teaching the power of the Holy Ghost, the enlightenment was awesome. That five foot two lady scared this six foot two strong man almost out of my skin. Her eyes looked like they were almost on fire. Her voice is usually soft and mild. But this time was different. She made her way toward me until she was about three feet away! She looked directly into my eyes. She was pointing directly toward me with her finger. In a very strong voice she spoke, "Don't tread on My Word!" I had received my answer. There was absolutely no way she had known what my wife and I had discussed in private. But God knows everything! It's silly to think He doesn't! Even the things we think are secret, just as Adam tried to hide behind a bush in the Garden of Eden.

The main thing He knows is our heart. And believe me, God's Word is real, alive, and true! It's a living Word. That means that today you may read verses in the Bible and not get much out of them. Then a year later, you may be going through something, and those same verses give you comfort and seem to have a different meaning. It is God's inspired, holy Word.

There many today who do not believe that you must be saved, then sanctified, then Holy Ghost filled. And they also don't believe you can live a sanctified, holy life. I can do all things through Christ Jesus! (See Philippians 4:13.) You may not believe me. I'm not upset with anyone who does not agree. You may be thinking, *Almost every Christian I know does not believe that!* Just because so many have the same opinion does not make it right! They thought the world was flat for centuries until Columbus proved them wrong. As for myself, I battle Satan every day in one form or another, and I get victory by the grace of God in Christ Jesus! I have been in controversy before I was ever born, as I had teenage parents in the late fifties. I've had to battle my way this far! So approval or disapproval either way will not damage my ego. I don't write for fame or fortune or ego. And I don't write for man's approval or the world's! God Almighty, the one who gave me life, wants this message to go out. So if God wants to wake me at all hours of the night, so be it. It's not a sacrifice; it's an honor! This book, this message, is God-driven, inspired, and needed! Even our advanced so-called intelligent society today needs correction! When puppies mean more than babies, and good is spoken evil of and evil is spoken highly of, we have a long way to go, and a short time to get there!

Now being saved, truly completely saved, a heartfelt saved, I don't go where I used to go, and I don't do what I used to do. I wanted more of God in my life! I now had new issues to face. But as all will find out, being saved does not stop the sin problem. It merely makes you more aware of sin in your life. When Jesus sets us free from sin, He also opens our eyes to the fact. Then we can go to the Father and pray for help in Jesus' name. Some believe you must bring your sins to the ordained priest to petition God's forgiveness. This is no longer required. You can go directly through Jesus to God. Some faiths claim you are to pay or do something for cleansing of sins, but Jesus has already paid the ultimate price! This gives us the ability to be free from sin without animal sacrifice.

But a problem still exists: we still sin!

For by grace are ye saved through faith; and that not of yourselves: it is the gift of God: Not of works, lest any man should boast. (Ephesians 2:8–9)

THE FALL OF MAN

Now the serpent was more subtle than any beast of the field which the LORD God had made. And he said unto the woman, Yea, hath God said, Ye shall not eat of every tree of the garden? And the woman said unto the serpent, We may eat of the fruit of the trees of the garden: but of the fruit of the tree which is in the midst of the garden, God hath said, Ye shall not eat of it, neither shall ye touch it, lest ye die. And the serpent said unto the woman, Ye shall not surely die: for God doth know that in the day ye eat thereof, then your eyes shall be opened, and ye shall be as gods, knowing good and evil. And when the woman saw that the tree was good for food, and that it was pleasant to the eyes, and a tree to be desired to make one wise, she took of the fruit thereof, and did eat, and gave also unto her husband with her; and he did eat.   (Genesis 3:1–6)

Satan deceived Eve, and then Eve convinced Adam to sin. When they disobeyed God, they sinned. This sin was bigger than eating a piece of fruit. This sin was not only against God but against humanity. Every sin man commits moves us further and further from civilization. And the acceptance of sin by man is works like a gravitational pull, pulling us straight down. It lowers our civility toward man. If you don't think we have a sin problem, watch the evening news in any major city.

We have a sin nature. It's in our DNA. People naturally sin. How did we get this sin nature?

When Adam and Eve ate the fruit, the pulp of the fruit was digested and passed. But a portion of the water (juice) was absorbed into their DNA. This physical DNA that was absorbed is passed from generation to generation. At the cross, many things happened:

1) The sins of the world were taken by our Savior, placed on Him so that through our confession to God we could be sin free.

2) We are able to become truly free, permanently holy. The command, *"Be holy, for I am holy"* (Leviticus 11:45), means to be separated from sin! But how can we accomplish that? When Jesus was on the cross, a soldier at His death pierced His side. Jesus was severely dehydrated. The angle from the ground, plus the fact that Jesus could not hold Himself up for He had given up the ghost means that the soldier pierced His side. I would estimate that he hit a rib, and the Bible says water and blood came out! The water that came out was a symbolic return of the water that had been in the fruit.

3) The blood was a symbolic return of the DNA, which represents our ability to be sanctified holy. As with salvation, the price has been paid. We only need to accept, and claim verbally that we are sanctified. This is done through a twofold sanctification. The first is progressive and is the separation from the daily press from sin, and the second is an instant work brought on by the Holy Ghost.

4) Upon Jesus' death, there was an opening in the spiritual realm for the complete power of the Holy Ghost to be manifested, making a path to receive the Holy Ghost in progression after sanctification has been achieved.

On the cross Jesus performed a miracle, the ability for us to be saved, sanctified, and Holy Ghost filled!

Note John 19:34:

But one of the soldiers with a spear pierced his side, and forthwith came there out blood and water.

SAVED. THEN SANCTIFIED

For those who believe that when you are saved, you have it all—you think you are saved, sanctified, and Holy Ghost filled. Are we better than our forefathers? I learn every day! A Christian serves God in the capacity He has chosen for you. He knows best! You are not meant only to sit on a bench on Sunday and sing songs, but you are to spread the gospel and the love of Jesus Christ through the entire world. Do you think Satan wants us Holy Ghost filled? The more power we have, the less he has.

But why do we need to be sanctified? We had been to a wonderful Sunday evening service. We had gone out of town to visit another church. On the way home, we were hungry. So we decided to stop for a burger. A national chain was the choice. As I was standing in line, a gentleman and I struck up a conversation. First, small talk; he had come in to get his son a burger. Oh, yes, we had just come from church. Where do we go to church? ECT. He then said, "I used to go to church, but I kept backsliding so I don't go anymore." At this point he got his food and left. As with many times in my life, I feel I should have done more, but the opportunity did not present itself. If I feel guilty now, how am I going to feel on judgment day?

Let's look at judgment day in the Old Testament Scriptures.

Surely as a wife treacherously departeth from her husband, so have ye dealt treacherously with me, O house of Israel, saith the Lord. A voice was heard upon the high places, weeping and supplications of the children of Israel: for they have perverted their way, and they have forgotten the Lord their God. Return, ye backsliding children, and I will heal your backslidings. Behold, we come unto thee; for thou art the Lord our God. Truly in vain is salvation hoped for from the hills, and

*from the multitude of mountains: truly in the LORD our God
is the salvation of Israel.* (Jeremiah 3:20–23)

The word *backsliding* means turning back or turning away
from.

*And I, brethren, could not speak unto you as unto spiritual,
but as unto carnal, even as unto babes in Christ. I have fed
you with milk, and not with meat: for hitherto ye were not
able to bear it, neither yet now are ye able. For ye are yet
carnal: for whereas there is among you envying, and strife,
and divisions, are ye not carnal, and walk as men?*
(1 Corinthians 3:1–3)

When we are saved, we are babes in Christ. And when the
sin problem will not depart, seek for and receive sanctification.

To be carnal means to be worldly in thought and to care
more about this world's matters and possessions more than
God! Does this sound like anyone you know?

*The backslider in heart shall be filled with his own ways:
and a good man shall be satisfied from himself.*
(Proverbs 14:14)

*But I say, that the things which the Gentiles sacrifice, they
sacrifice to devils, and not to God: and I would not that ye
should have fellowship with devils. Ye cannot drink the cup
of the Lord, and the cup of devils: ye cannot be partakers of
the Lord's table, and of the table of devils. Do we provoke
the Lord to jealousy? are we stronger than he?*
(1 Corinthians 10:20–22)

I pray all are able to grasp the revelations in this book. The
old paths brought us through. It's the old paths our forefathers

died for so we could know the way. When you sing any of the old hymns, did you feel the inspired blessing they contain?

UNCLEAN SPIRITS

When the unclean spirit is gone out of a man, he walketh through dry places, seeking rest, and findeth none. Then he saith, I will return into my house from whence I came out; and when he is come, he findeth it empty, swept, and garnished. Then goeth he, and taketh with himself seven other spirits more wicked than himself, and they enter in and dwell there: and the last state of that man is worse than the first. Even so shall it be also unto this wicked generation.
(Matthew 12:43–45)

That sounds like the state of the world today. When you go back on God, you are seven times worse off. Through sanctification, we don't have to go back. Use the same escape route I did. Anything that can control you must be removed before it becomes your God. How can I write about these things? That's easy. I experienced them firsthand. I've lived them. I will tell you straight, the only one telling me what to preach or teach is the Holy Ghost.

As for myself, I have watched person after person seeking at an altar of prayer, countless hours, for sanctification and then I have seen the change in their lives when they received it. Then I've watched them seek and receive the Holy Ghost. Seeing with your own eyes will make a believer out of you as it did me. When seeking, praying on my knees at an altar of prayer, a saint came over to pray for me. Afterward I said I would crawl under the carpet to be truly sanctified! I meant it! I was determined I could achieve the goal through fasting and prayer. After a lengthy session at the altar, I had prayed so hard I was soaking wet with sweat. As I stood up, my prayer partner, who had been by my side praying for me, looked at me. I stated, "Well, was it a boy or girl?" We both laughed only to break up the sadness of not receiving the blessing! I remember our pastor one time preaching that when you receive sanctification, even your dog and cat will know you have changed. I thought, yeah, right. Well, one day it happened at an altar of prayer! I was truly sanctified, and it changed my life forever. I was a new creature!

Maybe you don't think God can change you. My wife had smoked for many years. One day, she went to the altar of prayer and said, "Jesus, with Your help, I'm quitting!" She left her cigarette problem at the altar! I came home about two days later. She was on her knees, leaning over our ottoman and praying with tears flowing. She was free. No patch. No pills. No seven-step plan. Just one giant step, Jesus! She has been cigarette free ten years!

Let me give you another illustration. One day, my wife was walking the baby in the stroller, and a baby kitten that had been dropped off in the country was soon to have a new home. That cat and I did not have the best of friendships. I'm just thankful it was an outside cat. We called this beast Cricket because it loved to eat crickets. But it never liked me. It would stay just a few feet away. After receiving sanctification, this silly cat could not leave me alone. As we would sit on the deck, it would wind through my shins, rubbing and purring. That was just one more thing my pastor was right about! Why do we as humans try to place limits on a limitless God? Why does man try to outthink the Creator of thought! God still rules this universe!

If just a few more seek and receive the Holy Ghost power from God, it could possibly affect millions.

I do have a very interesting question for all saints. Some ministries teach that no one can be sanctified or Holy Ghost filled or sin free. Then what are they doing behind a podium preaching God's word? I will tell you this. If I was not right, there is absolutely no way I would get behind that sacred desk! The penalty would be too great to imagine!

That I should be the minister of Jesus Christ to the Gentiles, ministering the gospel of God, that the offering up of the Gentiles might be acceptable, being sanctified by the Holy Ghost. (Romans 15:16)

To open their eyes, and to turn them from darkness to light, and from the power of Satan unto God, that they may receive forgiveness of sins, and inheritance among them which are sanctified by faith that is in me. (Acts 26:18)

Jesus told the woman at the well, *"Go, and sin no more"* (John 8:11). Was He joking?

If so be that ye have heard him, and have been taught by him, as the truth is in Jesus: that ye put off concerning the former conversation the old man, which is corrupt according to the deceitful lusts; and be renewed in the spirit of your mind; and that ye put on the new man, which after God is created in righteousness and true holiness. (Ephesians 4:21–24)

Holiness is separation from sin. If you sin, you are forgiven, but you must resist sin. If you sin by omission, which means by default or mistake, ask for forgiveness! If you sin by commission, which means with knowledge or forethought, try sanctification. It worked for me and countless others.

As you look at all the verses on sanctification, think about this. If it was not important, then why would God Almighty place so much emphasis on it? And it seems ministries, at least the ones I have heard, don't talk about it!

First the definition (Webster's new world college dictionary 1988)

Sanctify 1) to make holy: to set apart as holy; consecrate b) To be free from sin; purify 2) to make binding or inviolable by a religious sanction 3) to make productive of spiritual blessing

Sanctified 1) dedicated; consecrated b) made holy

Put simply, holiness is separation from sin. To be sanctified is to be removed from sin and made holy by God.

OLD TESTAMENT VERSES

*And God blessed the seventh day, and **sanctified** it: because that in it he had rested from all his work which God created and made.* (Genesis 2:3)

*And Moses went down from the mount unto the people, and **sanctified** the people; and they washed their clothes.* (Exodus 19:14)

*And there I will meet with the children of Israel, and the tabernacle shall be **sanctified** by my glory.* (Exodus 29:43)

*And Moses took the anointing oil, and anointed the tabernacle and all that was therein, and **sanctified** them.* (Leviticus 8:10)

And he slew it; and Moses took the blood, and put it upon the horns of the altar round about with his finger, and puri-

*fied the altar, and poured the blood at the bottom of the altar, and **sanctified** it, to make reconciliation upon it.*

(Leviticus 8:15)

*And Moses took of the anointing oil, and of the blood which was upon the altar, and sprinkled it upon Aaron, and upon his garments, and upon his sons, and upon his sons' garments with him; and **sanctified** Aaron, and his garments, and his sons, and his sons' garments with him.*

(Leviticus 8:30)

*Then Moses said unto Aaron, This is it that the LORD spake, saying, I will be **sanctified** in them that come nigh me, and before all the people I will be glorified. And Aaron held his peace.* (Leviticus 10:3)

*And if he that **sanctified** it will redeem his house, then he shall add the fifth part of the money of thy estimation unto it, and it shall be his.* (Leviticus 27:15)

*And if he that **sanctified** the field will in any wise redeem it, then he shall add the fifth part of the money of thy estimation unto it, and it shall be assured to him.*

(Leviticus 27:19)

*And it came to pass on the day that Moses had fully set up the tabernacle, and had anointed it, and **sanctified** it, and all the instruments thereof, both the altar and all the vessels thereof, and had anointed them, and sanctified them.*

(Numbers 7:1)

For all the firstborn of the children of Israel are mine, both man and beast: on the day that I smote every firstborn in *the land of Egypt I **sanctified** them for myself.*

(Numbers 8:17)

*This is the water of Meribah, because the children of Israel strove with the LORD, and he was **sanctified** in them.*

(Numbers 20:13)

*Because ye trespassed against me among the children of Israel at the waters of Meribah-Kadesh, in the wilderness of Zin; because ye **sanctified** me not in the midst of the children of Israel.* (Deuteronomy 32:51)

*And the men of Kirjathjearim came, and fetched up the ark of the LORD, and brought it into the house of Abinadab in the hill, and **sanctified** Eleazar his son to keep the ark of the LORD.* (1 Samuel 7:1)

*And he said, Peaceably: I am come to sacrifice unto the LORD: sanctify yourselves, and come with me to the sacrifice. And he **sanctified** Jesse and his sons, and called them to the sacrifice.* (1 Samuel 16:5)

*And David answered the priest, and said unto him, Of a truth women have been kept from us about these three days, since I came out, and the vessels of the young men are holy, and the bread is in a manner common, yea, though it were **sanctified** this day in the vessel.* (1 Samuel 21:5)

*So the priests and the Levites **sanctified** themselves to bring up the ark of the LORD God of Israel.*

(1 Chronicles 15:14)

*For now have I chosen and **sanctified** this house, that my name may be there for ever: and mine eyes and mine heart shall be there perpetually.* (2 Chronicles 7:16)

*Then will I pluck them up by the roots out of my land which I have given them; and this house, which I have **sanctified** for my name, will I cast out of my sight, and will make it to be a proverb and a byword among all nations.*

(2 Chronicles 7:20)

*And they gathered their brethren, and **sanctified** themselves, and came, according to the commandment of the king, by the words of the LORD, to cleanse the house of the LORD.* (2 Chronicles 29:15)

*Now they began on the first day of the first month to sanctify, and on the eighth day of the month came they to the porch of the LORD: so they **sanctified** the house of the LORD in eight days; and in the sixteenth day of the first month they made an end.* (2 Chronicles 29:17)

*Moreover all the vessels, which king Ahaz in his reign did cast away in his transgression, have we prepared and **sanctified**, and, behold, they are before the altar of the LORD.*

(2 Chronicles 29:19)

*But the priests were too few, so that they could not flay all the burnt offerings: wherefore their brethren the Levites did help them, till the work was ended, and until the other priests had **sanctified** themselves: for the Levites were more upright in heart to sanctify themselves than the priests.*

(2 Chronicles 29:34)

*For they could not keep it at that time, because the priests had not **sanctified** themselves sufficiently, neither had the people gathered themselves together to Jerusalem.*

(2 Chronicles 30:3)

*Now be ye not stiffnecked, as your fathers were, but yield yourselves unto the LORD, and enter into his sanctuary, which he hath **sanctified** for ever: and serve the LORD your God, that the fierceness of his wrath may turn away from you.* (2 Chronicles 30:8)

*Then they killed the passover on the fourteenth day of the second month: and the priests and the Levites were ashamed, and **sanctified** themselves, and brought in the burnt offerings into the house of the LORD.* (2 Chronicles 30:15)

*For there were many in the congregation that were not **sanctified**: therefore the Levites had the charge of the killing of the passovers for every one that was not clean, to sanctify them unto the LORD.* (2 Chronicles 30:17)

*For Hezekiah king of Judah did give to the congregation a thousand bullocks and seven thousand sheep; and the princes gave to the congregation a thousand bullocks and ten thousand sheep: and a great number of priests **sanctified** themselves.* (2 Chronicles 30:24)

*And to the genealogy of all their little ones, their wives, and their sons, and their daughters, through all the congregation: for in their set office they **sanctified** themselves in holiness.* (2 Chronicles 31:18)

*Then Eliashib the high priest rose up with his brethren the priests, and they builded the sheep gate; they **sanctified** it, and set up the doors of it; even unto the tower of Meah they **sanctified** it, unto the tower of Hananeel.*
(Nehemiah 3:1)

*And all Israel in the days of Zerubbabel, and in the days of Nehemiah, gave the portions of the singers and the porters, every day his portion: and they **sanctified** holy things unto the Levites; and the Levites sanctified them unto the children of Aaron.* (Nehemiah 12:47)

*And it was so, when the days of their feasting were gone about, that Job sent and **sanctified** them, and rose up early in the morning, and offered burnt offerings according to the number of them all: for Job said, It may be that my sons have sinned, and cursed God in their hearts. Thus did Job continually.* (Job 1:5)

*But the LORD of hosts shall be exalted in judgment, and God that is holy shall be **sanctified** in righteousness.* (Isaiah 5:16)

*I have commanded my **sanctified** ones, I have also called my mighty ones for mine anger, even them that rejoice in my highness.* (Isaiah 13:3)

*Before I formed thee in the belly I knew thee; and before thou camest forth out of the womb I **sanctified** thee, and I ordained thee a prophet unto the nations.* (Jeremiah 1:5)

*I will accept you with your sweet savour, when I bring you out from the people, and gather you out of the countries wherein ye have been scattered; and I will be **sanctified** in you before the heathen.* (Ezekiel 20:41)

And say, Thus saith the Lord GOD; Behold, I am against thee, O Zidon; and I will be glorified in the midst of thee: and they shall know that I am the LORD, when I shall have executed *judgments in her, and shall be **sanctified** in her.*

(Ezekiel 28:22)

*Thus saith the Lord God; When I shall have gathered the house of Israel from the people among whom they are scattered, and shall be **sanctified** in them in the sight of the heathen, then shall they dwell in their land that I have given to my servant Jacob.*

(Ezekiel 28:25)

*And I will sanctify my great name, which was profaned among the heathen, which ye have profaned in the midst of them; and the heathen shall know that I am the Lord, saith the Lord God, when I shall be **sanctified** in you before their eyes.*

(Ezekiel 36:23)

*And thou shalt come up against my people of Israel, as a cloud to cover the land; it shall be in the latter days, and I will bring thee against my land, that the heathen may know me, when I shall be **sanctified** in thee, O Gog, before their eyes.*

(Ezekiel 38:16)

*When I have brought them again from the people, and gathered them out of their enemies' lands, and am **sanctified** in them in the sight of many nations.*

(Ezekiel 39:27)

*It shall be for the priests that are **sanctified** of the sons of Zadok; which have kept my charge, which went not astray when the children of Israel went astray, as the Levites went astray.*

(Ezekiel 48:11)

NEW TESTAMENT VERSES

*Say ye of him, whom the Father hath **sanctified**, and sent into the world, Thou blasphemest; because I said, I am the Son of God?* (John 10:36)

*And for their sakes I sanctify myself, that they also might be **sanctified** through the truth.* (John 17:19)

*And now, brethren, I commend you to God, and to the word of his grace, which is able to build you up, and to give you an inheritance among all them which are **sanctified**.* (Acts 20:32)

*To open their eyes, and to turn them from darkness to light, and from the power of Satan unto God, that they may receive forgiveness of sins, and inheritance among them which are **sanctified** by faith that is in me.* (Acts 26:18)

*That I should be the minister of Jesus Christ to the Gentiles, ministering the gospel of God, that the offering up of the Gentiles might be acceptable, being **sanctified** by the Holy Ghost.* (Romans 15:16)

*Unto the church of God which is at Corinth, to them that are **sanctified** in Christ Jesus, called to be saints, with all that in every place call upon the name of Jesus Christ our Lord, both theirs and ours.* (1 Corinthians 1:2)

*And such were some of you: but ye are washed, but ye are **sanctified**, but ye are justified in the name of the Lord Jesus, and by the Spirit of our God.* (1 Corinthians 6:11)

*For the unbelieving husband is **sanctified** by the wife, and the unbelieving wife is **sanctified** by the husband: else*

were your children unclean; but now are they holy.
(1 Corinthians 7:14)

*For it is **sanctified** by the word of God and prayer.*
(1 Timothy 4:5)

*If a man therefore purge himself from these, he shall be a vessel unto honour, **sanctified**, and meet for the master's use, and prepared unto every good work.* (2 Timothy 2:21)

*For both he that sanctifieth and they who are **sanctified** are all of one: for which cause he is not ashamed to call them brethren.* (Hebrews 2:11)

*By the which will we are **sanctified** through the offering of the body of Jesus Christ once for all.* (Hebrews 10:10)

*For by one offering he hath perfected for ever them that are **sanctified**.* (Hebrews 10:14)

*Of how much sorer punishment, suppose ye, shall he be thought worthy, who hath trodden under foot the Son of God, and hath counted the blood of the covenant, wherewith he was **sanctified**, an unholy thing, and hath done despite unto the Spirit of grace?* (Hebrews 10:29)

*Jude, the servant of Jesus Christ, and brother of James, to them that are **sanctified** by God the Father, and preserved in Jesus Christ, and called.* (Jude 1:1)

As you can see, much credence was given to sanctification. If this were not the case then countless millions of animals died for nothing. God called for the sacrifices! To be sin free was important then, and it is important now!

All leaders of the faith are to teach the Word of God cover to cover! This book is as an axe; it will cut as trees fall some toward, some away. It's simple. We are either moving closer to God, up, or we are moving farther away, down!

So what do all these stories and verses have to do with me? It's simple. God is not pleased. He has laid down a plan, a blueprint. It's rooted in Scripture, planted on the chief cornerstone. But today theologians, trying to outthink God, seem to think they have a better plan than God's! They go to great lengths to make members as comfortable as possible. The new attitude of the church is "you don't have to change." Have you ever been involved when a company buys another? They usually have a meeting to tell the employees, "Hey, nothing is going to change!" That's the only thing that doesn't change—the first lie!

God can't stand sin. He hates it! So to get closer to God and to be sin free, get sanctified! Faith gatherings should have certain sections: praise, worship, a message, Bible-based Scriptures, seeking, anointing with oil, baptism, prayer request, feet washing, communion fellowship, outreach, missionary, rebuking of demons, altar call, prayer for the sick. Should church be boring? No! If the Holy Ghost is in the house, believe me, it won't be boring!

New ideas. The world is more than ready to embrace the next great idea, no matter how bizarre it is. Just claim to be a professor, and people leap to believe in the next new idea. I'm beyond amazed at the extent of wrong thinking in this world as we seek to find the source of our problems. Most will embrace a falsehood before reality. Turn on the evening local news. Not all, but most that I have watched, make comments like, "Wow, that sure was a big storm that hit the Midwest,

Bill!" "It sure was. Old Mother Nature sure threw us a curve ball." My all time favorite was when I heard, "It sure has been dry. Well, we are going to see what we can do about it." When we view the weather people as if they were gods, we think they can predict the future and influence the temperature! My overall point is, who is Mother Nature? Can we go see her? Can we call? Does she have e-mail? We are so quick to embrace nonsense! It's not Mother Nature. Father God makes the weather!

We must try with love to help our fellow man see the truth. False teachings must be confronted with wisdom. We must stand for civility and values and help all to grasp a deeper understanding of our purpose here on earth. Life should not be a grab bag, and he who grabs the most is the winner! As children cry for food, as many are tortured, beaten, and starved or kept in submission, there is much work. God is calling! Are we listening?

The harvest is great, but the workers are few!

We are lacking knowledge and understanding. I've told this story before, but it needs to be repeated. One night while I was watching the evening news, the Creation vs. Evolution debate was the topic. The guests were a professed non-Christian and a Christian. The first guest said it was clear that man was created. The second, a Christian, stated that we evolved. He knew, because he was a science teacher. Let's see what the Holy Bible has to say about it! King James Bible. Chapter 1, verse 1. First page. First paragraph. *"In the beginning God created the heaven and the earth"* (Genesis 1:1).

That makes it pretty plain. This high school science teacher, a Christian, has been misled and is teaching others his faulty thinking. But a fever is not the sickness, only a symptom that something is wrong. Have we become so intelligent, so smart, that we know it all? We want to serve God only on our terms. This is a big mistake. The truths in the Bible are not up for debate.

Is the King James Bible infallible? Of course not. We need to all be on the same page. Not an uneducated or overeducated monster that rebels against Gods plan! God is the master. He rules and reigns in this and all universes! All evil will lose! Love will break the chains of bondage.

This comment the Christian made shows that he has a problem with the first page, first paragraph, first sentence, of the Holy Bible. We must pray for those who need to see the truth. The road may be hard and long. Disagreeing with God is a bad side of the road to find yourself on!

CHAPTER EIGHT

WASH ME, O LORD

I t was and is a revelation to me. I was writing a book about God's power and miracles. It was a Sunday night about 3:30 am. The day had been very eventful. My wife, being called of God, was ordained and now licensed by our pastor, bishop, and elder. Earlier that day, I had been watching a TV minister preach. He was talking about how important it is to be saved and baptized! Well, how did I miss that? I had missed a very important piece of what Jesus commanded!

When our Lord Jesus Christ had been resurrected, He came to His disciples and said,

All power is given unto me in heaven and in earth. Go ye therefore, and teach all nations, baptizing them in the name of the Father, and of the Son, and of the Holy Ghost: teaching them to observe all things whatsoever I have commanded you: and, lo, I am with you alway, even unto the end of the world. Amen. (Matthew 28:18–20)

WASH ME, O LORD

Colossians 2:8–9 says, *"Beware lest any man spoil you through philosophy and vain deceit, after the tradition of men, after the rudiments of the world, and not after Christ. For in him dwelleth all the fulness of the Godhead bodily."*

Any doctrine, philosophy, or new ideas that express views contrary to the Trinity—the Godhead—are deceit meant to pull power and purpose from Christ's church. The Enemy has many tricks to deceive and destroy as many of us as possible.

At 4:30 am, I must tell you, I had a combination of feelings. One thought was clear in my mind. The television and radio have a fair amount of teaching and preaching weekly. But we Christians let Christ down, when we don't do the works He has asked us to do. He did His part. Let me give you an example. I see crusade after crusade, millions saved. But when was the last time you have seen a baptism? I know a few people who claim to have read the whole Bible cover to cover. And that's great; some even read it twice per year. These are good things to do. But how many things did Jesus command us to do that we just ignore? How come so many miss the mark? We pick and choose which commands we want to follow. Let me spell it out plainly. People die every day. We spend most of our life in search of happiness. We go to school, we get jobs, we marry, have children, possibly grandchildren, then reality hits. Hey, I'm at the end of the road. For some, this revelation happens early, some later, some too late. The biggest decision of life is, Where do I spend eternity? I have tried to make it easy. Simply answer the multiple-choice quiz below. Please pick only one answer. Choose wisely. The time limit is only known by God. But I suggest, the sooner the decision is made the better. Some before us ran out of time.

Quiz Question: Where do you want to spend eternal life?

(Pick only one answer)

1) Choice one: Heaven. Streets of gold, rivers of living water, where you never get sick or die. Joy unspeakable and full of glory, a mansion high on a hill, a place so beautiful the human mind cannot comprehend.

2) Choice two: The Pit. Sheol, Hell, the lake of fire. An endless torture chamber, designed by God for Satan and his fallen rebellious angels. Where pain is never ending, where there is weeping and gnashing of teeth. Where one would beg for a drop of water to put the fire out on their tongue! And since you are a spirit, you cannot go into shock or die. You suffer forever and ever.

3) Choice three: Pick a faith other than Christianity: this puts you to answer #2!

4) Choice four: Make no decision at all. Just ignore the problem no matter what you have been taught. (Atheists usually choose this one. They say they don't have a position, but they are the ones trying to stop the pledge of allegiance, for example.) By proxy, you have chosen choice #2!

Which one did you pick? I will admit I'm a slow learner, but I eventually chose choice one. Some may need a few more years.

It seems most who have denied God suddenly receive a great revelation on their deathbed! Don't wait that long!

As I have said before, eternal life is not a choice! Where you spend it is!

WASH ME, O LORD

And fear not them which kill the body, but are not able to kill the soul: but rather fear him which is able to destroy both soul and body in hell. (Matthew 10:28)

I pray Jesus is your choice!

God and Jesus love you more than you will ever know!

This is he of whom I said, After me cometh a man which is preferred before me: for he was before me. And I knew him not: but that he should be made manifest to Israel, therefore am I come baptizing with water. And John bare record, saying, I saw the Spirit descending from heaven like a dove, and it abode upon him. And I knew him not: but he that sent me to baptize with water, the same said unto me, Upon whom thou shalt see the Spirit descending, and remaining on him, the same is he which baptizeth with the Holy Ghost. And I saw, and bare record that this is the Son of God. (John 1:30–34)

Jesus was first baptized to repentance (even though He was sin free), then God as a gift filled him with the Holy Ghost!

So again, baptism is very important! It's an outward showing of an internal change—an awesome change.

How close do you want to get?

How close?

Take a moment and think of this. You inherit your parents' old farmhouse. They inherited it from your grandparents. Times have been tough. It's one of your prize possessions. There is so much love there, so many memories. It has one very bad problem: the wiring is old and could catch fire any day. And now you cannot afford to replace the wiring. The nearest fire station is one hour away. The county wants to build a new one. When they have the meeting, they are going to want your opinion. They want feedback on how close to your house they should build the new firehouse! What do think? Forty-five minutes, thirty minutes, or how about five minutes? You have been almost afraid to leave home. So how close?

So now relate it to your soul, the only thing you take with you when you leave this earth. It is priceless, impossible to replace! How close do you want Jesus Christ to be? For me, as close as possible. For I don't want to burn.

CHAPTER NINE

THE VOICE, THE FAST, THE FILLING

As I do almost everyday, I was singing and praising God on my way to work. I had been praying and asking God for the same thing over and over again. He was probably getting tired of the same prayer. I will admit it. I was beginning to get a little frustrated. And I think that's where so many fail. God is not a drive-through God! He works in His own time, on His own agenda, not ours! We don't tell Him. He tells us. We pray and ask, and if it's in His will, we will receive. I believe that our prayers do not go out null and void! That these prayers come up before God as a testimonial. I had prayed and prayed and prayed. This morning was to be different! How different I could not have imagined!

I first need to make a point very clear. I think many times God could have been trying to tell me something, if I would be quiet enough to listen! For some, how is He going to get through? Look at so many, blaring music, cell phone almost glued to their head, and almost constant noise. How can He get your attention through the racket! Well as for myself, this particular morning, I was listening!

As I had said earlier, "Lord, how can I have a closer walk with You?" Then the voice came. It went right into me! It was unique, no-nonsense, strong but with a soft gripping quality. The voice said, "Do you want to get closer to Me? You will fast—I will tell you how and when!"

There was an anointing, a quickening inside me, so strong, that it was a wonder I was still driving. My reaction was a combination of screaming, "Hallelujah, praise God. Thank You, God," "Wow," and "Yes, Lord, all the way!" The Holy Ghost had just talked to me! This rejoicing continued. I praised all the way to work!

Upon arriving, I was so excited. This was one of the biggest events that ever happened in my life! I went around and said good morning and shook everyone's hand. They asked why I was so happy. I said, "God talked to me on the way to work!" I only wish I had a camera to capture their expressions. They thought I was nuts before, and this was the icing on the cake! They mostly just stared. A few said, "Well, that's nice," like you would say to a crazy person. It didn't matter. I was and still am one happy human!

God is true to His Word. In just a few days, the fasts had begun! First one, then another. As I'm writing this book, I'm on another fast. We serve an amazing God! There are many benefits to fasting that I will touch on later. At this point in our fasts, we have seen a spiritual gain and a weight loss. My weight had dropped from 272 pounds to 242 pounds.

There were many times I wondered how I was ever going to make it! Only through God's grace. At one point I became very weak. My shoes felt like those lead shoes deep-sea divers wear! Some would ask, "Carl, why aren't you eating?" I would say I was fasting. Don't worry about them. Most people don't even try to understand. It's easier to label someone a goof or nut instead of seeking the truth for themselves! I could write a book about that alone!

I was reminded of the weeks, months, and years that had passed by. As I watched God change person after person, I started to get that unhealthy attitude. How can that person receive the Holy Ghost? They just a few weeks ago testified they had a problem! Or an old time favorite, how can they get appointed deacon? I was here longer than them! You see it's the "God owes me something" attitude and pride that God hates! So we hold ourselves back. As for myself, I was not going to give up! I was reminded the spoken word is powerful! You see, earlier in my walk with the Lord I had said, "Lord, please don't give me the Holy Ghost if You are later going to take it away!" To receive such a special gift—the anointing power to serve—to lose this gift would be heartbreaking. Not to mention it would bring shame on myself!

It was a Sunday morning just like most. The fasts had left me feeling weak in body, but strong in spirit. For to whom much is given, much is required. My wife had purchased a new suit as a gift for me. Being new, the pants had not been hemmed so I wore the jacket with different pants. I also had on new dress shoes. You are probably thinking, why is he telling me this? Wait until you see what happens to my new suit! Church usually has a basic agenda, Sunday school, Bible study, then praise and worship, special singing, the message, then altar call, closing. After Sunday school, we started to gather up front as usual. The pastor stated we were first going to have prayer for those sick in body. As is scriptural, the elders and deacons would pray as the pastor would anoint with oil.

This is usually done by placing one or two drops on his finger, then placing on the forehead. I had gone up to receive prayer for a missing member. Our pastor, a great man of God, has helped our family many times. Not to get too sidetracked, but I feel I must tell this story. After a weeklong revival, my wife became very ill. Not from the revival I might add. This was a complication from a previous operation. I had rushed her to the emergency room. On the way I had called the pastor to ask for prayer. He was not home, so I left him a message filling him in. It was about 10:30 pm. Instead of just praying for her from home, the pastor and his wife came to the emergency room! They came in with an upbeat spirit. They stayed at least an hour. I knew the pastor was tired, and he gets up very early in the morning. Their love was stronger than their need to rest. You see some people play Christian, some live the true life, a dedicated service to others, showing the true love of Christ! God's glory will shine through those filled with the Holy Ghost and others He touches at His will.

RECEIVING THE GIFT OF THE HOLY GHOST

The pastor had prayed over me. I humbly stepped back. The praise and worship started. I had started singing along. Then something started to happen. Something I had never experienced before. A feeling of very strong anointing, as if an electrical force was flowing through me! It started near my stomach, and then it moved into my back, then down both legs. That is the only way to describe just some of the energy going through me. Have you ever seen a crew on a flight deck, on an aircraft carrier? Their clothes blow in the wind, a high speed flapping. Well, just imagine that my legs inside my pants were flapping. I mean the muscles were moving. I was hit with power—real power! Earthshaking power. If there wasn't so much joy, I would have been scared to death. Let me tell you firsthand, God's power is nothing to joke about or to play with. The next thing I knew I was wobbling back and forth, side to side. Then bam, on the floor I went! I was kicking uncontrollably. I turned on my side and did a complete 360, like one of those old comedies, or so I was told. I eventfully ended up on my back, and I was speaking in tongues, an unknown uncontrollable language. I knew that much. What I was saying, only God knows. I will tell you it was not anything anyone had taught me. All I knew was that the Holy Ghost was speaking through me. Hallelujah, I was filled, and I mean Holy Ghost filled.

Those few minutes changed my life forever!

As I lay there praising God, the tears were flowing down my face until my collar on my shirt was getting wet. Thank You, God, thank You, God! I was holding my hands up. After a few minutes, I started to notice the music. What a blessing. While on my back, I had kicked uncontrollably. That had subsided. Things were calm, but inside of me had been placed a fire! A desire, a fresh new power to serve. If I had ever wanted to do more for God, I now had the power and approval to do it. This does not mean that I'm better then anyone else. I'm still just a servant of Christ! God has power to give all saints, but do they want it? I mean really want it. It could mean coming out of their comfort zone, a fast, praying for someone in public. Or even not being politically correct!

Do you want the power! Really! There are plenty of big talkers! Hey, I was a big talker! God has changed me, an awesome change! God is awesome!

When I finally made it back to my feet, the tears were flowing and I was praising God. After a short while, the music stopped. When the power of God is falling, many headed to the altar for prayer or deliverance. God's power cuts off chains of bondage. So many had received a blessing, but I was the only one filled with the Holy Ghost that day. The music finally stopped. The pastor said, "Carl, do you have something to say?" I could barely speak! This next sentence is very important: words are powerful and important when you receive a spiritual gift. You should speak it if God saves you, sanctifies you, or fills you with the Holy Ghost. Tell God how much you appreciate it, and tell the devil you have moved up and to back off! With that much power still going through me. I composed myself, and spoke. "I will serve God until the day I die."

These were wonderful words, but I had not claimed the gift. I had forgotten a very important part. I went back to the pew happy. The pastor delivered the message, God's message. Then altar call was given. This means the altar is open to all. Deacons and prayer partners pray for all that need prayer. I went up to thank God for the gift. I also could have done this in my seat, but the altar is a humbling spot. As we said our good-byes, the pastor said, "Carl, did I hear you speak in tongues?" That was his way of saying, "You did not claim the gift."

Before we left, I took a tissue and removed the scuffmarks from my feet kicking the carpet while I was on my back.

We left to drive home. As we were driving, the Holy Ghost spoke to me in my spirit. "Tonight you will testify and proclaim that you have received the baptism of the Holy Ghost."

We go to service on Sunday evenings on a regular basis. I waited and waited to testify about the gift. It was finally at the very end of the service. I did not want to be disobedient. The pastor said, "Does anybody else have anything to say?"

As I stood up to speak, my body was trembling. But there was another voice, a different voice, saying, "Sit down. You will look like a fool! You should have told them this morning. Now they won't believe you." Satan was trying to stop me, but it was too late. You must press through. I stood up and said, "Yes, I do! This morning I was so overwhelmed by God's power, I missed something! I wanted to proclaim that this morning I received the gift of the filling of the Holy Ghost!" The Holy Ghost rose up in me. I twisted and shook from my head to my toes. I could barely sit down. I could tell by faces and responses, some believed, some did not. If you want to serve God in any capacity, and expect everyone to be happy, think again. This is a one-on-one relationship with God. If your goal is to be a man pleaser, you are already on the wrong road. Please God, or you may be crying, "God, please." I was not going to let the reaction of a few steal my joy. Words can't always describe every event in life. Some things must be experienced!

I don't remember exactly when I noticed, but when I looked in the mirror, something was different besides a smile on my face. I did a double take. I was born with brown eyes with a little touch of green. God had changed my eye color from brown to green, with a very little brown, almost unnoticeable. God changed my eye color. You see, He is not only the Creator; He is the Re-creater. As He has changed the outside and inside of me, He wants to do the same for you! Spiritual gifts are for the seekers. Ask, seek, and knock. I thanked God for changing my eyes. It was spoken into my spirit, "If I wanted to make them blue, I could have!" I said, "Make them blue, God. Make them whatever You want!"

A little earlier in my walk, I had been troubled. A wise brother in Christ asked if I was okay. I said I was having problems, but I was going to press my way through, but sometimes I didn't feel like I was pleasing to the Lord. He said, "Is He talking to you, son?" I said, "Yes." He said, "Then you will be alright!"

So now when different ones come along and want to debate the Holy Ghost, I have something easy to say to them. Argue with my eyes!

CHAPTER TEN

THE ARMOR OF GOD

We are in a battle! Some may be surprised to hear it. Many today live in flat land, completely unaware of the worlds around them! We battle ourselves for an understanding of our own purpose, then to understand world events, finances, family events, solar events. Then here comes a whole new arena, the spiritual battle!

So how did we get into this spiritual battle anyway?

We were born into this battle. As man drew his first breath, his adversary was already making plans for his downfall. Lucifer, a powerful angel, had what he thought was a bright idea! He conspired to overthrow God Himself! His plan failed, but not before he had convinced one third of the angels in heaven to follow him. God threw him and them out of heaven. Satan had dominion over earth until man showed up. When Adam and Eve, through rebellion, ate the forbidden fruit, they basically handed the keys of earth over to Satan (his fallen name). Jesus returned the keys back to humans. These keys are spiritual. For the record, some claim Satan can read our minds! If Satan could read anyone's mind, it would have been Christ's.

If Satan had any idea Jesus would be that powerful and set man free, Jesus would have never made it to the cross, believe me! It is our big mouths that get us into trouble! We speak our own demise. I have made the mistake to speak of how I hate inventory. So Satan helps me out. It seems no matter where I work, I always get stuck doing inventory!

THIS BATTLE

The apostle Paul said it brilliantly.

For we wrestle not against flesh and blood, but against principalities, against powers, against the rulers of the darkness of this world, against spiritual wickedness in high places.
(Ephesians 6:12)

Principalities   (Webster's dictionary)

1) The rank, dignitary, or jurisdiction of a prince

2) The territory ruled by a prince.

3) A country with which a princes title is identified

The Prince of Darkness is Satan himself!

POWER

The ability to control other authority, special authority assigned to or exercised by a person or group holding office

A spirit or divinity, an armed force, army, navy, military strength (Air power)

Powers—Authority, spirits, an army, air power

Let's size up the factors.

Evil—Darkness

First, we fight against ourselves from Adam and Eve until today.

Satan

The prince of darkness

Wickedness in high places

Wickedness in low places

Promoters of sin, abortion, entrapment, imprisonment, murder, genocide, hatred, evil, rebellion.

Promoters of anarchy, mental cruelty, sex offenders, sex abusers, adulterers, racists, demons, imps, fallen angels.

Any attackers of the true Word of God, the Ten Commandments, haters and killers of Christian and Jews

Goodness—Light

God the Father, God the Son, God the Holy Ghost

Angels, cherubim, all saints, saved, sanctified and Holy Ghost-filled

The Jews

Now greater is He that is with us, but if you add all the divisions, denominations, and other factors into account, we need God more than ever! But just remember this: God has never been defeated! The devil has.

Rulers of Darkness:

Any ruler or person of authority that permits Satan or satanic powers influence his or her judgment. Anyone who imposes Satan's will on the people. Any law or judgment that directly comes up against God or the Ten Commandments!

And I'm not playing politics. Facts are facts! Satan uses rulers to promote wickedness in his own interest. There is spiritual wickedness in high and low places. We have plenty to fight!

So what do we have that will help us to stand? It's not what we have; it's what God can give us.

Wherefore take unto you the whole armour of God, that ye may be able to withstand in the evil day, and having done all, to stand. Stand therefore, having your loins girt about with truth, and having on the breastplate of righteousness; and your feet shod with the preparation of the gospel of peace; above all, taking the shield of faith, wherewith ye shall be able to quench all the fiery darts of the wicked. And take the helmet of salvation, and the sword of the Spirit, which is the word of God: praying always with all prayer and supplication in the Spirit, and watching thereunto with all perseverance and supplication for all saints; and for me, that utterance may be given unto me, that I may open my mouth boldly, to make known the mystery of the gospel, for which I am an ambassador in bonds: that therein I may speak boldly, as I ought to speak. (Ephesians 6:13–20)

THE ARMOR

1) Loins girt with truth

2) Breastplate of righteousness

3) Feet shod with the gospel of peace

4) The shield of faith

5) The helmet of Salvation

6) The sword of the Spirit

If you read carefully, you'll see that the areas of the body that are covered are the loins, chest, feet, front, head, and a sword is given for attack. What area is left vulnerable? You've got it—your back!

First, as Christians, we are triumphant! We should always be moving forward. Face your enemy. We are on God's side! God does not retreat or turn back!

Beware the enemy uses many! And it seems even those close to you! Well-wishers, even some who claim to serve the Lord? The Russians have an expression, Trust but verify. Be quite careful who can get close enough to thrust a spiritual dagger in your back.

We must pray and talk to God on a steady basis, we must sup, commune with the spirit. Stay on the mission God has placed us on.

And they were all filled with the Holy Ghost, and began to speak with other tongues, as the Spirit gave them utterance. (Acts 2:4)

What was Paul saying? "God, even though I have the armor, I need power!" The power of the Holy Ghost to give me a powerful word of utterance and what makes us bold. The anointing, the Holy Ghost.

The Armor of God has six pieces. The Holy Ghost is one piece. Together, they are the complete package, all seven pieces.

Believe me, this was a revelation to me, and I have shared it as it was given to me. I was surprise and enlightened.

We need the whole package! Seven pieces.

One more major point. What is the battle over? Souls!

The mission I am on and other ministers, pastors, bishops, cardinals, and saints should all be the same. For if we fail, the blood of the lost will be on our hands! For those who don't think studying and praying and helping others is not important, it's sad to think you won't have anyone to stand in for you on judgment day! We fight for civilization itself!

Evaluate your enemy. We must be prepared to face the enemy! Is the potential threat or attack qualified to do harm to our person or spirit or country? If left unattended will it go away? Did Goliath go away? Did the Kaiser in WWI, or Hitler in WWII? We must learn from David he ran to go address Goliath! Why? Simple. He knew that if he waited Satan would try to weaken his spiritual strength! Our enemies test our resolve to see if we will run to or from our problems! As Hitler was appeased and pampered, Japan was ignored, which lead to Pearl Harbor. Pointing fingers at appointments will not make them go away! As Christians, if we don't stand with power, the whole world will pay a price! Backing down to worldly enemies is potential death. Losing the spiritual battle is possible eternal torture. Make the right choice. Put on the whole armor of God!

CHAPTER ELEVEN

FASTING

Many people don't understand the role and function of fasting. They believe there is only one kind of fast, and that is to have absolutely nothing. Not even water. In this chapter, I will show you what God actually says about fasting.

Why do we fast? God knows our body. As we fast many things happen. Our body spends much energy and time digesting food. While fasting, our body can work on repairing other areas. A very important part is when we fast, if we pray we will gain spiritual strength. Why? We get our flesh under subjection. When our flesh tells us to get out of bed and get something to eat, who's in control? Are we or is our flesh? Anything that tries to come between you and God is becoming your god! We must get control of our mind and our body.

Fasting is like giving. Everyone in town doesn't have to know you're fasting. When you fast, it should only be evident to your spouse or other immediate family.

Moreover when ye fast, be not, as the hypocrites, of a sad countenance: for they disfigure their faces, that they may appear unto men to fast. Verily I say unto you, They have their reward. But thou, when thou fastest, anoint thine head, and wash thy face; that thou appear not unto men to fast, but unto thy Father which is in secret: and thy Father, which seeth in secret, shall reward thee openly.

(Matthew 6:16–18)

And when they were come to the multitude, there came to him a certain man, kneeling down to him, and saying, Lord, have mercy on my son: for he is a lunatic, and sore vexed: for ofttimes he falleth into the fire, and oft into the water. And I brought him to thy disciples, and they could not cure him. Then Jesus answered and said, O faithless and perverse generation, how long shall I be with you? how long shall I suffer you? bring him hither to me. And Jesus rebuked the devil; and he departed out of him: and the child was cured from that very hour. Then came the disciples to Jesus apart, and said, Why could not we cast him out? And Jesus said unto them, Because of your unbelief: for verily I say unto you, If ye have faith as a grain of mustard seed, ye shall say unto this mountain, Remove hence to yonder place; and it shall remove; and nothing shall be impossible unto you. Howbeit this kind goeth not out but by prayer and fasting.

(Matthew 17:14–21)

In Old Testament times, even the animals were put on fasts, along with the humans. John the Baptist ate locusts and wild honey!

I was in a shopping club store. In the rear of the store, ladies handing out samples of different types of food. One lady said, "Try mine." I said, "No, thank you." She said, "Don't you like it?" I liked it, but I explained very softly that I was fasting and that I was going to try the other lady's shrimp instead. She said immediately, "When you fast, you eat or drink nothing!" I could feel the Holy Ghost's presence was getting strong. I said, "Ma'am, if God told you, through the Holy Ghost, not to eat sugar or fat for three days, what would you do?" She said, "Obey God." I gently placed my hand on her shoulder. I said, "That's what's wrong today. Many people today claim they want a closer walk with God. But they want it on their terms! People run for man's advice and approval before seeking God's!" We both rejoiced as I left because she was also a Christian. I had never met her before. Then we went about our shopping, and yes the shrimp were good.

Have you noticed the Christian world and the secular world are quick to place Christians and God in a box! You can't do that! You can't do this! Anti-Christian factions around the world are quick to label us troublemakers, as they murder and destroy! "Free Barabbas," they cried. "Kill Jesus. He's the troublemaker!" Well, I'm striving to be Christlike. So if helping others or feeding the needy or praying for the sick will be a crime, I am guilty as charged. Satan was behind the mob to kill Jesus, and it's this very same Satan that is behind the anti-Christian, anti-Jew movement happening this very day! But I have some news, hot off the presses. God Almighty runs and owns this and all the universes!

I must make this point clear. God Almighty can call a fast at any time. Most of my fasts have been a deletion of certain items, and others have been absolutely nothing! Seek God for His will for you. It's a one-on-one relationship!

CHAPTER TWELVE

THE NEW BATTLEGROUND

Or should I say same old battleground, different tactics!

How can the Christian faith be beaten? Easy. With the oldest trick in the book, the one that worked from the very beginning—division! It worked with Adam and Eve, and it still works today. What I find that is amazing, although God did warn them, Adam and Eve didn't know any better. They had never been deceived before. Satan, the master deceiver, took care of them in short order. But we have so many intelligent, educated, and learned individuals. We're prepared. There's absolutely no way Satan can fool us. Ha! It's been easier for him than he probably thought! So what's the master plan of the deceiver?

Simple as mashed potatoes and gravy!

1) Divide us into as many denominations as possible!

Demonstrations: to detonate to make divisions, a portion!

More divisions means less unity. As for our faith, our motto should be "united we stand," just as it is for our country.

2) Just as with Adam and Eve, Satan twists the Word of God.

He alters it a little here and a little there. How does he accomplish this? How many new Bibles are there? And when many preach, are they preaching out of the Bible, or just telling stories or ideas. I love a good story, don't you? Something soft and fuzzy. But it's not appropriate for church. I would hate to think how many could spiritually starve to death waiting on a word from God!

Ministry is very simple; either you preach what God wants you to preach, or what you want. When you preach in self, you are saying, "God, I don't need Your input. I can do it on my own!" The problem when you preach in self is that you are denying God's power! It is God's power that breaks off the yokes of bondage.

Today's Christian faith has also developed some traits that Christ would not be so proud of. It seems that when one falls, the rest can't wait to trample the fallen one to the ground with their mouths! As soon as one falls, the mouths start. Did you hear about so and so? Let's try something new and try praying for them! Pray for God to show mercy. Pray for God to intervene. God's grace is sufficient for the day each and every day! We need each other. It was never intended to be this way. We are meant to be united!

When did God lose His power? Never!

Then why is it that today's so-called holy churches don't have more power than ever? We think we're at a new level where we don't need to fast, pray, baptize, have feet washing, take communion, have altar calls or testimony services, ask forgiveness, or waste our time on such technicalities like sanctification or seeking for the indwelling of the Holy Ghost! Even though Jesus commanded each one—and He also said much more! So why have so many churches lost so much power? They have altered God's Word to exclude the power of the Holy Ghost!

Let's compare some Scriptures from that old King James Bible, then some of the same verses from one of the new Bible translations.

We will examine three random verses.

First the new Bible, *New King James Version.*

*Above all, taking the shield of faith with which you will be able to quench all the fiery darts of the **wicked one**.*
(Ephesians 6:16 NKJV, emphasis added)

Now the King James Version of Ephesians 6:16:

*Above all, taking the shield of faith, wherewith ye shall be able to quench all the fiery darts of the **wicked**.*
(emphasis added)

Are we fighting the evil one or all evil! We are fighting all the wicked! Is one word important?

In the *New King James Version,* it says, "you," while the King James says, "ye." Why would one word change a meaning?

You is self-explanatory. Webster's Dictionary defines ye as "dialectical speech as accusative singular and plural." *Ye* means all Christians, you and me!

See the difference?

Let's look at another one.

*Go therefore and **make** disciples of all the nations, baptizing them in the name of the Father and of the Son and of the **Holy Spirit**.*   (Matthew 28:19 NKJV, emphasis added)

*Go ye therefore, and **teach** all nations, baptizing them in the name of the Father, and of the Son, and of the **Holy Ghost**.*   (KJV, emphasis added)

Let's look at the phrase, "make disciples of all nations." Is that of Christ? Jesus didn't *make* me love Him. I chose Him after learning and feeling His love, mercy, and forgiveness, and feeling His presence. Have you ever tried to make someone love you? You can't! Jesus said to *teach*, not make.

In the holy Spirit/Holy Ghost question, upon completion of salvation, one's spirit would be holy at that point, until we sin again. The doctrine of "when you're saved you have it all" is false. You have just taken your first step toward spiritual fulfillment.

The Holy Ghost a gift from God, separate from salvation. In the following Scriptures, you will see what happens when someone tries to outthink the Scriptures! Inserting Holy Spirit in place of Holy Ghost, nice try.

Look at the *New King James Version* of Acts 19:1–6:

And it came to pass, that, while Apollos was at Corinth, Paul having passed through the upper coasts came to Ephesus: and finding certain disciples, he said unto them, Have ye received the Holy Ghost since ye believed? And they said unto him, We have not so much as heard whether there be any Holy Ghost. And he said unto them, Unto what then were ye baptized? And they said, Unto John's baptism. Then said Paul, John verily baptized with the baptism of repentance, saying unto the people, that they should believe on him which should come after him, that is, on Christ Jesus. When they heard this, they were baptized in the name of the Lord Jesus. And when Paul had laid his hands upon them, the Holy Ghost came on them; and they spake with tongues, and prophesied.

So which side of the street are we going to walk on? Salvation is not given by the laying on of hands. I don't know anyone who when saved prophesied and spoke in tongues!

Do you see the difference with your own eyes? The deception!

I'm not a commissioned sales representative for the King James Bible. I'm just trying to show the deception and what I see with love.

One Sunday evening we were watching a TV minister preach. He used three different Bibles. How can you read and follow? If you can't follow them in Scripture, don't follow them!

We don't need others to tell us, "Don't worry. Take my word for it."

How many innocent Jewish men, women, and children went into the gas chambers being told it's only a shower. Don't tell me, show me!

The Pharisees and scribes kept the Holy Scriptures in the temple. They told the law!

The Bible is not to be hidden or dished out in portions or to be kept secret! The Bible is for everyone!

Are we admitting we have a decreased level of intelligence that we need to be talked to like little babies! In high school, my reading levels were low. I had to take special reading classes to improve my speed and comprehension. But you don't have to give me a special Bible so I can understand the words.

THE TEN COMMANDMENTS

If a person calls a book holy and it's not based on the Ten Commandments—where the basics of sin comes from as instructed by God Himself and separation from sin being holiness—this book cannot be called a Holy Bible. For if God had intended other books to be holy they would be based on the Ten Commandments. The Holy Bible is not to be changed, not one word. Woe unto the doer!

As many have died for the faith, do we think God is playing? He's only going to tolerate so much, as some misguided teachers deny His power and then alter His Holy Word. We can now consider ourselves warned!

The King James Version is the Holy Bible.

King James gathered forty-seven of the brightest scholars and painstakingly had each word translated in the Holy Bible. The Old Testament was translated from Hebrew, and the New Testament from Greek. It took them seven years! Why? So everyone could have a Bible, God's Word! At first I was skeptical! Many have died for our freedom and right to choose. The new Bibles claim they are trying to help readers to discover the Bible in a new and exciting way! How sweet and thoughtful. It will be exciting all right, when the church is powerless! I will admit with all these helpers, life soon will be so easy. Things are getting so mentally predigested. I mean, we wouldn't want to hurt our brain getting to the truth, now would we? The world is quick to tell us what it wants us to hear. I don't know about you, but as for me, tell it to me straight whatever it is! God's Word, the news, everything, let me make the informed decision! Did you ever wonder why Jesus taught in parables? To make the disciples use their brains. To think of things in the realms of natural and spiritual! When you read the Bible, pray for God to enlighten you. If Satan can get us on different Bibles, and keep us from being in one accord, he can block some of our power! Notice I did not say all. For God can rise up who He wills to carry on. We must stand up for what is right and accept the power that is rightly ours and put Satan in his place. One God, one Jesus, one Holy Ghost! One Bible—the King James Version. One mind, one accord, leads to power! Not make believe, but real power!

It was a new morning! I was blessed. I had a special meeting to go to so this sunny beautiful morning, I could leave home a little later than usual. My wife and I were talking. She said there was a Bible teacher on television. I'd like to watch him. But when the Bible says Holy Ghost, he says Holy Spirit. I can't watch him. God's Word is just that—His holy Word. For the record, no other faith can have a holy book! Why? Simple. Holiness is separation from sin. What is a sin? Breaking one of the Ten Commandments. If a faith claims to be holy and does not follow the Ten Commandments, they can't be holy! You see the English language is simple. It's in English! No holiness, no holy book. It's just that simple. Anyone who doesn't like it can take it up with God. He made the rules! But here's the bigger question. It arises over and over again! Why do preachers, pastors, bishops, and a host of others—educated, learned, doctors—why do they preach what is not in the Holy Bible?

I made it a point to ask, "Is there a fine for saying Holy Ghost on TV or radio?" So far I've heard no. But just to be safe, I may save a few dollars just in case! I'm sure a few get uneasy hearing Holy Ghost! Could it be that they don't have a clue about the most powerful force in all the universes! And to explain is too complicated. I mean, it's so easy to tell everyone when you get saved, you have it all! And then ask for an offering! If anyone gets uneasy with Holy Ghost, they should be as uneasy with saying God or Jesus! For they are one!

For the record there is a fine for changing God's Holy Word.

And, behold, I come quickly; and my reward is with me, to give every man according as his work shall be. I am Alpha and Omega, the beginning and the end, the first and the last. Blessed are they that do his commandments, that they may have right to the tree of life, and may enter in through the gates into the city. For without are dogs, and sorcerers, and whoremongers, and murderers, and idolaters, and whosoever loveth and maketh a lie. I Jesus have sent mine angel to testify unto you these things in the churches. I am the root and the offspring of David, and the bright and morning star. And the Spirit and the bride say, Come. And let him that heareth say, Come. And let him that is athirst come. And whosoever will, let him take the water of life freely. For I testify unto every man that heareth the words of the prophecy of this book, If any man shall add unto these things, God shall add unto him the plagues that are written in this book. (Revelation 22:12–18)

(Note: I hope everybody understands the severity of changing God's Holy Word. No second chances!)

So with our new best helpers rewriting the Bible, how about this idea: get saved, and claim you have it all! Why not? Is that what Jesus commanded? He has offered a gift of the Father! The Holy Ghost!

How many times do I hear Holy Spirit? Let's look at the Scriptures for clarification.

The spirit of the LORD   (1 time)

Holy Spirit of God   (1 time)

The Spirit of God   (26 times)

The Holy Ghost (90 times)

If I miscounted, please forgive me!

Don't you think by accident someone would preach or teach on the Holy Ghost? Well, you don't have to worry. This book is to serve notice! God will raise up willing vessels that will! As for me, I have already had the discussion with my wife. I will either preach the truth of God's Word or die trying!

Why do so many refuse God's power ?

Did you wonder what "The Spirit of God" means?

Hereby know ye the Spirit of God: Every spirit that confesseth that Jesus Christ is come in the flesh is of God.

(1 John 4:2)

Now, let's look at holy Spirit.

But they rebelled, and vexed his holy Spirit: therefore he was turned to be their enemy, and he fought against them. Then he remembered the days of old, Moses, and his people, saying, Where is he that brought them up out of the sea with the shepherd of his flock? where is he that put his holy Spirit within him? (Isaiah 63:10–11)

Who is the Great Shepherd? When we ask for salvation, He awakens our spirit within. So here's the big question. Why would anyone preach what is not in the Bible and then not preach what is in the Bible? Are they trying to be man pleasers? Well, then things are just repeating themselves! The Sadducees and the Pharisees in Acts 5 brought forth Peter and the apostles to trial for preaching the truth of the gospel and the Holy Ghost.

Then the high priest rose up, and all they that were with him, (which is the sect of the Sadducees,) and were filled with indignation, and laid their hands on the apostles, and put them in the common prison. But the angel of the Lord by night opened the prison doors, and brought them forth, and said, Go, stand and speak in the temple to the people all the words of this life. And when they heard that, they entered into the temple early in the morning, and taught. But the high priest came, and they that were with him, and called the council together, and all the senate of the children of Israel, and sent to the prison to have them brought. But when the officers came, and found them not in the prison, they returned, and told, saying, The prison truly found we shut with all safety, and the keepers standing without before the doors: but when we had opened, we found no man within. Now when the high priest and the captain of the temple and the chief priests heard these things, they doubted of them whereunto this would grow. Then came one and told them, saying, Behold, the men whom ye put in prison are standing in the temple, and teaching the people. Then went the captain with the officers, and brought them without violence: for they feared the people, lest they should have been stoned. And when they had brought them, they set them before the council: and the high priest asked them, saying, Did not we straitly command you that ye should not teach in this name? and, behold, ye have filled Jerusalem with your doctrine, and intend to bring this man's blood upon us. Then

Peter and the other apostles answered and said, We ought to obey God rather than men. The God of our fathers raised up Jesus, whom ye slew and hanged on a tree. Him hath God exalted with his right hand to be a Prince and a Saviour, for to give repentance to Israel, and forgiveness of sins. And we are his witnesses of these things; and so is also the Holy Ghost, whom God hath given to them that obey him.

(Acts 5:17–32)

Look at verse 32, "*The Holy Ghost, whom God hath given to them that obey him.*"

Do you have to do anything special to get saved? Simply repent in Jesus' name with a repentant heart. We're not talking about getting saved. But Holy Ghost indwelling is different.

If it is of God, it will stand!

Let's look again. Verse 29 says we ought to obey God rather than men. Verse 32 says the Holy Ghost is witness and is given to them that obey God.

Man pleasers are not God pleasers!

God pleasers are given the Holy Ghost at God's will, in God's time, and at God's discretion.

So a huge, but simple question to answer is, Do you think God is pleased when His written Word is altered? Do you think He is pleased when the Holy Ghost, a precious gift, is left out of many churches? The Holy Ghost—one-third of the Godhead!

*Forasmuch then as we are the offspring of God, we ought not to think that the **Godhead** is like unto gold, or silver, or stone, graven by art and man's device.*

(Acts 17:29, emphasis added)

God, Jesus, and the Holy Ghost are more precious than gold, silver, or anything we can imagine or build!

And the times of this ignorance God winked at; but now commandeth all men every where to repent.   (verse 30)

God's patience is wearing thin. How much longer will He wink at our disobedience?

Why don't others seek His gift of the Holy Ghost? Well, unlike salvation, the Holy Ghost and santifacitation, you have to actually work at it! I mean pray, fast, seek, and knock. Go into your spiritual closet.

It is a fact that anything you want to keep together you have to work for! Marriage, family, home, etc. If you don't, they will simply fall apart! Do you think God is happy with a weakened church?

That's why God has me writing this book.

Study Acts 7:51:

Ye stiffnecked and uncircumcised in heart and ears, ye do always resist the Holy Ghost: as your fathers did, so do ye.

This makes it crystal clear! Acts was written in 62 AD, but this verse could have been written yesterday! Who are we to resist the Holy Ghost?

THE GODHEAD AND THE JUDGMENT

As Christians, we should all know that when the breath leaves the body we will be judged. Our Lord will intercede to the Father.

Jesus Himself said in Matthew 10:32-33,

Whosoever therefore shall confess me before men, him will I confess also before my Father which is in heaven. But whosoever shall deny me before men, him will I also deny before my Father which is in heaven.

So Jesus said, "Deny Me, and I will deny you!"

The Godhead is comprised of God the Father, God the Son, and God the Holy Ghost. They are three, but they are one!

Note: The following is how Satan can stop us from entering into heaven!

Is heaven a sure thing? It should be a no-brainer. But Satan is slick. If he can get you to deny any part of the Godhead, Jesus must deny you before the Father! This is not my opinion, but scriptural fact! If you don't like it, just think how many burn right now for denying the Holy Ghost! Look, I did not make it up; it's in the Bible!

There's a knock at the door. It's someone you have been expecting. You greet them, "Hi, come in, but leave your leg outside. Come on in, but leave your head outside." It sounds ridiculous. Just think of how the fad of saying Holy Spirit in place of Holy Ghost is taken by God!

Fact: When we are judged, if we have denied the Holy Ghost, Jesus must deny us before the Father!

We were in a store where a young couple was selling cosmetics. The couple was very nice. They were Americans, but the product came from Israel. We said we love to support Israel. They stated they were Christians. My youngest son said, "Do you know about the Holy Ghost?" He's getting as bad as his father! Anyway, they said, "You mean Holy Spirit!" He said, "No, Holy Ghost. They're different." He explained, "Like cupcakes and cake are both cakes, but there is a difference!"

I thought I would fall over! He then sung them a song! What wisdom from a seven year old!

It's amazing a seven year old gets it! So I don't think it's impossible for everyone else. I'm not trying to be ugly, just factual!

The summation is God gave us His Son, His holy Word, and His Holy Ghost! Today very few even mention the words. And don't hold your breath waiting to hear how to receive the gift. And believe me it's a gift. I'm also saddened that leaders of the faith have let our power base slip away! Where we don't need old paths or old Bibles.

We have a new plan. We know best. Yeah, right! This misrepresentation of God's holy Word will provoke God's wrath. Does Satan have that much power? Well, he's taking it away day by day. I used to watch certain TV ministries and weep from the anointing; now I watch and weep from the lack of anointing. Mega churches, you think one would say, "Excuse me, pastor, could you tell me what Holy Ghost means?" On the day of Pentecost, three thousand souls were added in one day! They did not have TV or radio, cable, satellite, just word of mouth. Many today in the faith do wonderful things. This book is not a book of judgment. It's to be a book of enlightenment for those who can open their mind to receive it. Miracle working power can be yours. Not for your use, but for God's.

I love Jesus, what He has done and who He is. I don't want to see one soul lost! Not even one. To break demonic powers, we need God's power in our lives. The gifts of the Holy Ghost!

BLESSING ROBBERS

I used to attend a holiness church. At the end of service, the pastor would ask, "With heads bowed, all that want to be saved come now to an altar of prayer. Now all those who want to be sanctified holy come. And those that are seeking the baptism of the Holy Ghost come now." This was done, for each individual was proclaiming without speaking what they were seeking for.

You will find power in your words and actions. With faith we are more than conquerors.

As we seek to grow, is Satan just going to stand by and just let it happen? Hardly!

We were having a tent revival. I was excited having been on fasts. I thought this was it! The music and anointing were awesome! Was this going to be my night to receive the Holy Ghost?

It was the second or third night. My expectation was high. I could feel the presence of the Holy Ghost pulling me to the altar! As altar call was given. I went up the anointing was awesome! I felt as though I was going to be filled! I now will show you where the title blessing blockers comes from. I had noticed as the tent revival progressed, more and more unusual looking guests were arriving. Some testifying, some praising! Some just left me wondering. One man stood and testified, "There are only two churches in this area like this, and they are the only two still standing!" My thoughts were was he proclaiming good or would they be the next to fall?

I proceeded to the altar, as I said. I was down on my knees, my mind reminding me of hearing of another brother's testimony of how he was filled at a tent revival! This was it! Just then, an event I could not foresee happened. The man that testified earlier almost ran to the altar. He took both his hands and pushed down on my back—so hard it drove my face into my hands. He may have said bless him, but his violence was not of God! He left. I arose and said to one of the ushers, "Hey, are you watching what is going on? I was almost mugged at the altar!" I'm not blaming that man for myself not receiving the gift. What I'm saying is that he distracted my prayer and focus! Satan wants us to lose focus! If God has something for you, it's for you!

Another story, we were having a revival. A gentleman had recently started attending church. He claimed he had the Holy Ghost! He was very well versed on the Bible. He had acquired this education in prison. I don't have a problem with the fact he was in prison. He was coming on a regular basis and sitting in the back. We were having a great revival. I have been in a church where the presence of God manifested by the Holy Ghost was so strong, everyone just sat in their pews and wept and then most fell out in the spirit! This one particular Sunday, an altar call was given. Many came forward to seek. The power of the Holy Ghost was awesome! All of a sudden, this man came up front screaming, "That's not how I got it! Down on my knees! Well, if that's the way you want to do it, well alright!" He had been trying to break the spirit. Satan will use those who will let him! Beware of blessing robbers. These are people being used by Satan thinking they're doing well! But the end result breaks the spirit of worship and blessing!

Why did I say robber? For a thief steals when we are not looking. But a robber will steal in front of your face. Don't let Satan do this to you!

CHAPTER THIRTEEN

THE GIFT

The greatest gift ever given in the history of man has already been given! Our heavenly Father gave us salvation and the forgiveness of sins. This came as a result of a very costly price, His only begotten Son Jesus!

The Holy Ghost is a precious gift, and it's just that. Money can't buy gift.

But when they believed Philip preaching the things concerning the kingdom of God, and the name of Jesus Christ, they were baptized, both men and women. Then Simon himself believed also: and when he was baptized, he continued with Philip, and wondered, beholding the miracles and signs which were done. Now when the apostles which were at Jerusalem heard that Samaria had received the word of God, they sent unto them Peter and John: who, when they were come down, prayed for them, that they might receive the Holy Ghost: (For as yet he was fallen upon none of them: only they were baptized in the name of the Lord Jesus.) Then laid they their hands on them, and they received the Holy Ghost. And when Simon saw that through laying on of the apostles' hands the Holy Ghost was given, he offered them money, saying, Give me also this power, that on whomsoever I lay hands, he may receive the Holy Ghost. But Peter said unto him, Thy money perish with thee, because thou hast thought that the gift of God may be purchased with money. Thou hast neither part nor lot in this matter: for thy heart is not right in the sight of God. Repent therefore of this thy wickedness, and pray God, if perhaps the thought of thine heart may be forgiven thee. For I perceive that thou art in the gall of bitterness, and in the bond of iniquity. Then answered Simon, and said, Pray ye to the Lord for me, that none of these things which ye have spoken come upon me.

(Acts 8:12–24)

How do you receive a gift? Do you make someone give you a gift? Do you force someone to give a gift?

When did God's blessings stop? Never! Have we as a body of Christ just simply stopped seeking, trying, and asking for the gift? As for myself, I'm not the holiness police! With so many ministers not even saying *Holy Ghost,* are some trying to be people pleasers?

Then Peter and the other apostles answered and said, We ought to obey God rather than men. (Acts 5:29)

Is that part of the problem, that we are too worried about the world? The other reasons could include being uneducated or feeling uncomfortable even saying the words! As we run out of excuses, there is one many seem to pass by: Satan and his attempt to stop the teaching of the Holy Ghost!

If God's Word, my words, and the Scriptures are not enough, get out a phone book, look up holiness churches, call a few, and ask do you teach on the Holy Ghost? If they say yes, then ask if the presence of the Holy Ghost has fallen on a regular basis? If they answer yes, take a Sunday or two and go to that church. Watch and feel the presence for yourself! As I have said, God did not put the words Holy Ghost in the Bible ninety times for nothing! Let's look at the Scriptures. Take your Bible, and please read the Scriptures before and after these.

> *Now the birth of Jesus Christ was on this wise: When as his mother Mary was espoused to Joseph, before they came together, she was found with child of the* **Holy Ghost**.
> (Matthew 1:18)

> *But while he thought on these things, behold, the angel of the Lord appeared unto him in a dream, saying, Joseph, thou son of David, fear not to take unto thee Mary thy wife: for that which is conceived in her is of the* **Holy Ghost**.
> (Matthew 1:20)

> *I indeed baptize you with water unto repentance: but he that cometh after me is mightier than I, whose shoes I am not worthy to bear: he shall baptize you with the* **Holy Ghost**, *and with fire.*
> (Matthew 3:11)

> *Wherefore I say unto you, All manner of sin and blasphemy shall be forgiven unto men: but the blasphemy against the* **Holy Ghost** *shall not be forgiven unto men. And whosoever speaketh a word against the Son of man, it shall be forgiven him: but whosoever speaketh against the* **Holy Ghost**, *it shall not be forgiven him, neither in this world, neither in the world to come.*
> (Matthew 12:31–32)

> *Go ye therefore, and teach all nations, baptizing them in the name of the Father, and of the Son, and of the* **Holy Ghost**.
> (Matthew 28:19)

*I indeed have baptized you with water: but he shall baptize you with the Holy **Ghost**.* (Mark 1:8)

*But he that shall blaspheme against the **Holy Ghost** hath never forgiveness, but is in danger of eternal damnation.* (Mark 3:29)

*For David himself said by the **Holy Ghost**, The LORD said to my Lord, Sit thou on my right hand, till I make thine enemies thy footstool.* (Mark 12:36)

*But when they shall lead you, and deliver you up, take no thought beforehand what ye shall speak, neither do ye pre-meditate: but whatsoever shall be given you in that hour, that speak ye: for it is not ye that speak, but the **Holy Ghost**.* (Mark 13:11)

*For he shall be great in the sight of the Lord, and shall drink neither wine nor strong drink; and he shall be filled with the **Holy Ghost**, even from his mother's womb.* (Luke 1:15)

*And the angel answered and said unto her, The **Holy Ghost** shall come upon thee, and the power of the Highest shall overshadow thee: therefore also that holy thing which shall be born of thee shall be called the Son of God.* (Luke 1:35)

*And it came to pass, that, when Elisabeth heard the salutation of Mary, the babe leaped in her womb; and Elisabeth was filled with the **Holy Ghost**.* (Luke 1:41)

*And his father Zacharias was filled with the **Holy Ghost**, and prophesied.* (Luke 1:67)

HOLY GHOST AND FIRE, HOLY GROUND

And, behold, there was a man in Jerusalem, whose name was Simeon; and the same man was just and devout, waiting for the consolation of Israel: and the **Holy Ghost** *was upon him. And it was revealed unto him by the* **Holy Ghost**, *that he should not see death, before he had seen the Lord's Christ.* (Luke 2:25–26)

John answered, saying unto them all, I indeed baptize you with water; but one mightier than I cometh, the latchet of whose shoes I am not worthy to unloose: he shall baptize you with the **Holy Ghost** *and with fire.* (Luke 3:16)

And the **Holy Ghost** *descended in a bodily shape like a dove upon him, and a voice came from heaven, which said, Thou art my beloved Son; in thee I am well pleased.* (Luke 3:22)

And Jesus being full of the **Holy Ghost** *returned from Jordan, and was led by the Spirit into the wilderness.* (Luke 4:1)

And whosoever shall speak a word against the Son of man, it shall be forgiven him: but unto him that blasphemeth against the **Holy Ghost** *it shall not be forgiven.* (Luke 12:10)

For the **Holy Ghost** *shall teach you in the same hour what ye ought to say.* (Luke 12:12)

And I knew him not: but he that sent me to baptize with water, the same said unto me, Upon whom thou shalt see the Spirit descending, and remaining on him, the same is he which baptizeth with the **Holy Ghost**. (John 1:33)

*(But this spake he of the Spirit, which they that believe on him should receive: for the **Holy Ghost** was not yet given; because that Jesus was not yet glorified.)* (John 7:39)

*But the Comforter, which is the **Holy Ghost**, whom the Father will send in my name, he shall teach you all things, and bring all things to your remembrance, whatsoever I have said unto you.* (John 14:26)

*And when he had said this, he breathed on them, and saith unto them, Receive ye the **Holy Ghost**.* (John 20:22)

*Until the day in which he was taken up, after that he through the **Holy Ghost** had given commandments unto the apostles whom he had chosen.* (Acts 1:2)

*For John truly baptized with water; but ye shall be baptized with the **Holy Ghost** not many days hence.* (Acts 1:5)

*But ye shall receive power, after that the **Holy Ghost** is come upon you: and ye shall be witnesses unto me both in Jerusalem, and in all Judaea, and in Samaria, and unto the uttermost part of the earth.* (Acts 1:8)

*Men and brethren, this scripture must needs have been fulfilled, which the **Holy Ghost** by the mouth of David spake before concerning Judas, which was guide to them that took Jesus.* (Acts 1:16)

*And they were all filled with the **Holy Ghost**, and began to speak with other tongues, as the Spirit gave them utterance.* (Acts 2:4)

*Therefore being by the right hand of God exalted, and having received of the Father the promise of the **Holy Ghost**, he hath shed forth this, which ye now see and hear.* (Acts 2:33)

*Then Peter said unto them, Repent, and be baptized every one of you in the name of Jesus Christ for the remission of sins, and ye shall receive the gift of the **Holy Ghost**.*

(Acts 2:38)

*Then Peter, filled with the **Holy Ghost**, said unto them, Ye rulers of the people, and elders of Israel.*   (Acts 4:8)

*And when they had prayed, the place was shaken where they were assembled together; and they were all filled with the **Holy Ghost**, and they spake the word of God with boldness.*   (Acts 4:31)

*But Peter said, Ananias, why hath Satan filled thine heart to lie to the **Holy Ghost**, and to keep back part of the price of the land?*   (Acts 5:3)

*And we are his witnesses of these things; and so is also the **Holy Ghost**, whom God hath given to them that obey him.*   (Acts 5:32)

*Wherefore, brethren, look ye out among you seven men of honest report, full of the **Holy Ghost** and wisdom, whom we may appoint over this business.*   (Acts 6:3)

*And the saying pleased the whole multitude: and they chose Stephen, a man full of faith and of the **Holy Ghost**, and Philip, and Prochorus, and Nicanor, and Timon, and Parmenas, and Nicolas a proselyte of Antioch.*   (Acts 6:5)

*Ye stiffnecked and uncircumcised in heart and ears, ye do always resist the **Holy Ghost**: as your fathers did, so do ye.*   (Acts 7:51)

THE GIFT

*But he, being full of the **Holy Ghost**, looked up stedfastly into heaven, and saw the glory of God, and Jesus standing on the right hand of God.* (Acts 7:55)

*Who, when they were come down, prayed for them, that they might receive the **Holy Ghost**.* (Acts 8:15)

*Then laid they their hands on them, and they received the **Holy Ghost**. And when Simon saw that through laying on of the apostles' hands the **Holy Ghost** was given, he offered them money, saying, Give me also this power, that on whomsoever I lay hands, he may receive the **Holy Ghost**.* (Acts 8:17–19)

*And Ananias went his way, and entered into the house; and putting his hands on him said, Brother Saul, the Lord, even Jesus, that appeared unto thee in the way as thou camest, hath sent me, that thou mightest receive thy sight, and be filled with the **Holy Ghost**.* (Acts 9:17)

*Then had the churches rest throughout all Judaea and Galilee and Samaria, and were edified; and walking in the fear of the Lord, and in the comfort of the **Holy Ghost**, were multiplied.* (Acts 9:31)

*How God anointed Jesus of Nazareth with the **Holy Ghost** and with power: who went about doing good, and healing all that were oppressed of the devil; for God was with him.* (Acts 10:38)

*While Peter yet spake these words, the **Holy Ghost** fell on all them which heard the word. And they of the circumcision which believed were astonished, as many as came with*

111

*Peter, because that on the Gentiles also was poured out the gift of the **Holy Ghost**.* (Acts 10:44–45)

*Can any man forbid water, that these should not be baptized, which have received the **Holy Ghost** as well as we?*
(Acts 10:47)

*And as I began to speak, the **Holy Ghost** fell on them, as on us at the beginning.* (Acts 11:15)

*Then remembered I the word of the Lord, how that he said, John indeed baptized with water; but ye shall be baptized with the **Holy Ghost**.* (Acts 11:16)

*For he was a good man, and full of the **Holy Ghost** and of faith: and much people was added unto the Lord.*
(Acts 11:24)

*As they ministered to the Lord, and fasted, the **Holy Ghost** said, Separate me Barnabas and Saul for the work whereunto I have called them.* (Acts 13:2)

*So they, being sent forth by the **Holy Ghost**, departed unto Seleucia; and from thence they sailed to Cyprus.*
(Acts 13:4)

*Then Saul, (who also is called Paul,) filled with the **Holy Ghost**, set his eyes on him.* (Acts 13:9)

*And the disciples were filled with joy, and with the **Holy Ghost**.* (Acts 13:52)

*And God, which knoweth the hearts, bare them witness, giving them the **Holy Ghost**, even as he did unto us.*
(Acts 15:8)

*For it seemed good to the **Holy Ghost**, and to us, to lay upon you no greater burden than these necessary things.*
(Acts 15:28)

*Now when they had gone throughout Phrygia and the region of Galatia, and were forbidden of the **Holy Ghost** to preach the word in Asia.*
(Acts 16:6)

*He said unto them, Have ye received the **Holy Ghost** since ye believed? And they said unto him, We have not so much as heard whether there be any **Holy Ghost**.*
(Acts 19:2)

*And when Paul had laid his hands upon them, the **Holy Ghost** came on them; and they spake with tongues, and prophesied.*
(Acts 19:6)

*Save that the **Holy Ghost** witnesseth in every city, saying that bonds and afflictions abide me.*
(Acts 20:23)

*Take heed therefore unto yourselves, and to all the flock, over the which the **Holy Ghost** hath made you overseers, to feed the church of God, which he hath purchased with his own blood.*
(Acts 20:28)

*And when he was come unto us, he took Paul's girdle, and bound his own hands and feet, and said, Thus saith the **Holy Ghost**, So shall the Jews at Jerusalem bind the man that owneth this girdle, and shall deliver him into the hands of the Gentiles.*
(Acts 21:11)

*And when they agreed not among themselves, they departed, after that Paul had spoken one word, Well spake the **Holy Ghost** by Esaias the prophet unto our fathers.*
(Acts 28:25)

*And hope maketh not ashamed; because the love of God is shed abroad in our hearts by the **Holy Ghost** which is given unto us.* (Romans 5:5)

*I say the truth in Christ, I lie not, my conscience also bearing me witness in the **Holy Ghost**.* (Romans 9:1)

*For the kingdom of God is not meat and drink; but righteousness, and peace, and joy in the **Holy Ghost**.* (Romans 14:17)

*Now the God of hope fill you with all joy and peace in believing, that ye may abound in hope, through the power of the **Holy Ghost**.* (Romans 15:13)

*That I should be the minister of Jesus Christ to the Gentiles, ministering the gospel of God, that the offering up of the Gentiles might be acceptable, being sanctified by the **Holy Ghost**.* (Romans 15:16)

*Which things also we speak, not in the words which man's wisdom teacheth, but which the **Holy Ghost** teacheth; comparing spiritual things with spiritual.* (1 Corinthians 2:13)

*What? know ye not that your body is the temple of the **Holy Ghost** which is in you, which ye have of God, and ye are not your own?* (1 Corinthians 6:19)

*Wherefore I give you to understand, that no man speaking by the Spirit of God calleth Jesus accursed: and that no man can say that Jesus is the Lord, but by the **Holy Ghost**.* (1 Corinthians 12:3)

The Gift

*By pureness, by knowledge, by longsuffering, by kindness, by the **Holy Ghost**, by love unfeigned.*   (2 Corinthians 6:6)

*The grace of the Lord Jesus Christ, and the love of God, and the communion of the **Holy Ghost**, be with you all. Amen.*   (2 Corinthians 13:14)

*For our gospel came not unto you in word only, but also in power, and in the **Holy Ghost**, and in much assurance; as ye know what manner of men we were among you for your sake.*   (1 Thessalonians 1:5)

*And ye became followers of us, and of the Lord, having received the word in much affliction, with joy of the **Holy Ghost**.*   (1 Thessalonians 1:6)

*That good thing which was committed unto thee keep by the **Holy Ghost** which dwelleth in us.*   (2 Timothy 1:14)

*Not by works of righteousness which we have done, but according to his mercy he saved us, by the washing of regeneration, and renewing of the **Holy Ghost**.*   (Titus 3:5)

*God also bearing them witness, both with signs and wonders, and with divers miracles, and gifts of the **Holy Ghost**, according to his own will?*   (Hebrews 2:4)

*Wherefore (as the **Holy Ghost** saith, To day if ye will hear his voice.)*   (Hebrews 3:7)

*For it is impossible for those who were once enlightened, and have tasted of the heavenly gift, and were made partakers of the **Holy Ghost**.*   (Hebrews 6:4)

Holy Ghost and Fire, Holy Ground

*The **Holy Ghost** this signifying, that the way into the holiest of all was not yet made manifest, while as the first tabernacle was yet standing.* (Hebrews 9:8)

*Whereof the **Holy Ghost** also is a witness to us.* (Hebrews 10:15)

*Unto whom it was revealed, that not unto themselves, but unto us they did minister the things, which are now reported unto you by them that have preached the gospel unto you with the **Holy Ghost** sent down from heaven; which things the angels desire to look into.* (1 Peter 1:12)

*For the prophecy came not in old time by the will of man: but holy men of God spake as they were moved by the **Holy Ghost**.* (2 Peter 1:21)

*For there are three that bear record in heaven, the Father, the Word, and the **Holy Ghost**: and these three are one.* (1 John 5:7)

*But ye, beloved, building up yourselves on your most holy faith, praying in the **Holy Ghost**.* (Jude 1:20)

Jesus, in His own words, said,

He that loveth me not keepeth not my sayings: and the word which ye hear is not mine, but the Father's which sent me. These things have I spoken unto you, being yet present with you. But the Comforter, which is the Holy Ghost, whom the Father will send in my name, he shall teach you all things, and bring all things to your remembrance, whatsoever I have said unto you. (John 14:24–26)

Do the new Bibles keep His sayings? How about the Word or teachings? And could it be possible that some are so booked learned that, because they think they know it all, they actually deny the simplicity of God's plan? We have merely scratched the surface of study and understanding on this subject! I pray that all will grasp the revelation before it's too late.

> *How God anointed Jesus of Nazareth with the Holy Ghost and with power: who went about doing good, and healing all that were oppressed of the devil; for God was with him. And we are witnesses of all things which he did both in the land of the Jews, and in Jerusalem; whom they slew and hanged on a tree: him God raised up the third day, and showed him openly; not to all the people, but unto witnesses chosen before of God, even to us, who did eat and drink with him after he rose from the dead. And he commanded us to preach unto the people, and to testify that it is he which was ordained of God to be the Judge of quick and dead. To him give all the prophets witness, that through his name whosoever believeth in him shall receive remission of sins. While Peter yet spake these words, the Holy Ghost fell on all them which heard the word. And they of the circumcision which believed were astonished, as many as came with Peter, because that on the Gentiles also was poured out the gift of the Holy Ghost. For they heard them speak with tongues, and magnify God. Then answered Peter, Can any man forbid water, that these should not be baptized, which have received the Holy Ghost as well as we? And he commanded them to be baptized in the name of the Lord. Then prayed they him to tarry certain days.* (Acts 10:38–48)

In this story, we clearly see the gift of the Holy Ghost. The gift was given, then they were baptized. Another miracle was that the Gentiles also received. God poured out the gift and they spoke in tongues, which is just one more sign that one has the indwelling of the Holy Ghost. God is still pouring out the gift.

Man's opinion of himself may actually hinder him from receiving the gifts God had planned for him. There is absolutely no reason that demons should not moan as we approach them, but some might think, "Well, as the apostles did, you have the Holy Ghost, so you can drink deadly things etc." Look, when God takes any of us home, it's at His discretion, but to think we are immune to death or sickness is ridiculous. God's power can deliver us out of any circumstance, but it is not wise to tempt the Lord your God!

Let's look at these special gifts.

1) Speaking in tongues

2) Interpretation

3) Prophecy

4) Discernment of Spirits

5) Wisdom

6) Knowledge

7) Healing

8) Miracles

Are these gifts at work in your place of worship? There isn't any reason why they should not be!

SPEAKING IN TONGUES

*"They were all filled with the Holy Ghost, and began to speak with other tongues, **as the Spirit gave them utterance**"* (Acts 2:4, emphasis added). I heard a TV minister say that speaking in

tongues is just like speaking any other language that you can control. Where did he get that?

Speaking in tongues is an act of submission to the Holy Ghost. If you are in control of your vocal cords, the Holy Ghost is not! When I speak in tongues, it's from submission. And how can I teach you something that comes up out of me uncontrollably! And woe unto the ones trying to teach a version of tongues that comes very close to blasphemy! Don't play with God!

INTERPRETATION OF TONGUES

The interpretation of tongues is the God-given ability to hear and interpret messages given by the Holy Ghost while speaking in tongues. This is a very special gift of which I do not have much to write. The reason being from what I know this gift is very rare. But for the doubting Thomases of the world, just because you have not heard or seen doesn't mean it doesn't exist.

PROPHECY

Prophecy is a foreknowledge of world or personal events also revelation of events as shown by the Holy Ghost. It is foretelling events through divine revelation and also a prophetic or divine word spoken over someone.

DISCERNMENT OF SPIRITS

The discernment of spirits is the ability to perceive, detect, and have inner knowledge or detection of evil spirits or demonic activity.

Beloved, believe not every spirit, but try the spirits whether they are of God: because many false prophets are gone out into the world. Hereby know ye the Spirit of God: Every spirit that confesseth that Jesus Christ is come in the flesh is of God: and every spirit that confesseth not that Jesus Christ is come in the flesh is not of God: and this is that spirit of antichrist, whereof ye have heard that it should come; and even now already is it in the world.   (1 John 4:1–3)

Also beware of soothsayers—one who pretends to foretell the future for money and is of false praise!

Daniel answered in the presence of the king, and said, The secret which the king hath demanded cannot the wise men, the astrologers, the magicians, the soothsayers, show unto the king; but there is a God in heaven that revealeth secrets, and maketh known to the king Nebuchadnezzar what shall be in the latter days. Thy dream, and the visions of thy head upon thy bed, are these.   (Daniel 2:27–28)

God knows and owns the future!

The Holy Ghost sees and hears and detects supernatural behavior before we do. Our spiritual self inside us is ultra sensitive. How do I know? Our pastor was preaching one day, and as he spoke at a certain part of the message, he spoke, "Who out there wants to go back to where they were when they were in sin?" Those words cut like a razor right into the very depth of my soul. Before he finished the whole sentence, a tear ran down my check. I had not even time to cry; my spirit inside wept! Our inner being is that sensitive.

MALL TIME

My wife had asked me to go shopping. She's a super lady and though I deeply love her, shopping is not what I would consider a joy! I hate the thought of looking for who knows what, who knows where, for hour upon hour. It's almost like an Easter egg hunt in tall grass, but we're not sure anyone put eggs out there.

To give this story justice, we must go back seven or eight years. My wife had met a young lady, very nice. My wife was going to witness to her. She was surprised to find that the young lady was trying to convert *her* to a new group of faith that was only partially based on biblical truth. In this faith, they believe Jesus is God's Son but not the Messiah. I don't even waste my time on such idiotic ideas! But one thing I did notice from a piece of their literature was that Jesus was depicted on a stick with nails, not a cross! As a Christian, my Savior died on a cross, not on a stick. He is the Savior of the world, not a popsicle on a stick! The cross represents the Holy Trinity! I warned my wife to be very careful with these people. Our God is greater, but stay away from evil. This young lady even sent her pastor hoping to convert us, but to no avail!

Now we fast forward to about eight months ago. My wife found a few things, so I bought them for her. And being tall, I volunteered to carry her dress to keep it from hitting the ground. As we went through a set of big glass doors, a couple was coming in. The man had on an unusual hat, and I wondered where I had seen that hat before. He said to my wife, "Would you like a tract?" (A tract is a little booklet with pictures and usually Scriptures.) My wife said thank you, thinking maybe she would receive some nice Scriptures. Was I about to get a surprise!

My wife reached for it as they passed, and they went into the store. The heavy doors closed in seconds. My wife no sooner had it in her hand than I said, "Throw it away, throw it away!" There was a trash can right there. She had glanced to see who it was from. I had not even seen who it was from. But the Holy Ghost knew! Oh boy, did He know! The Holy Ghost knew before I did. My spiritual being knew before my carnal man. As I stepped out the door into the parking lot, the Holy Ghost had taken over and I was speaking in tongues. There was an open rebuke of Satan for about five minutes! I will tell you when that power hits you, I don't care who is standing in front of you! You don't care who or what hears you! When the Holy Ghost takes over, submit! As I wrote this story I remembered where I had seen that hat before. That same style hat was worn by that pastor that came by our house years earlier. I had forgotten, but God hadn't!

And for the record, don't waste your time on those who want to play church. Eternity is a long time to burn for following the wrong leader. Choose wisely! Make sure they're following Christ!

AT THE MALL AGAIN

About one month after the first incident, we had gone by the mall to visit a chain restaurant. They were featuring new items on their menu. We asked the hostess, "May we please not sit by the bar?" After our second table move, we had enough. We decided to go to another chain that features all the salad you care to eat. I think you know which one. So we proceeded to leave. At a minimal distance was a young lady. She had two children, one in a stroller that I estimated to be two or three years old. She and the children were dressed in black. I don't hate black clothes. There is a point I want to make clear: when I see bizarre clothing or behavior, in most cases, I simply go about my business. She, if I remember, had a lot of piercings, and her clothes had a lot of unusual writing on it. It did not take more than a second to notice the satanic cross she displayed on the shirt, and I'm not an expert on satanic anything! Again, things that are contrary or evil, I try to look away from, but she and her children were headed straight for us. I tried to give her room. The Holy Ghost inside me rose up like a fireball! The Holy Ghost knew the writings. He recognized them straight off, and as I walked past her on the way to the van, the Holy Ghost took control. I was speaking in tongues and walking in the spirit (an almost total control of one by the Holy Ghost). The Holy Ghost spoke through me. To this day I do not remember all the words that were spoken. To the best of my memory, I said, "How bold, Satan. How bold you are to spread your filth! I know you. Your day of judgment comes soon!" Then more tongues. Then more rebuke.

By that time we had arrived at the other restaurant. Things had begun to calm down. My mother-in-law was not surprised. She has seen God perform many wondrous works in her life. Only God knows if the young lady understood what had happened. I know this: Satan is a black hole; get too close, and he will suck you in. And unless you have a heart change, you are hellbound! The occult, Satan, evil, black magic—are people ever going to learn? How much love do you need to get right?

WISDOM

Wisdom is the quality of being wise, the ability to judge, also the ability to apply judgment based on experience!

When one receives the Holy Ghost, God may at His discretion give a larger portion thereof!

KNOWLEDGE

Knowledge is a state of knowing, intelligence, and understanding, to be grasped by the mind, enlightenment, a body of facts.

God enlightens at His will.

MIRACLES

A miracle is an event or events that defy standard or perceived norms. God has never stopped being in the miracle business. In my first book, a book of hope and miracles that I wrote in prayer under God, I shared the following story.

MY BABY'S MIRACLE

Our smallest child was born a week or so late. From his first examinations, our pediatricians expressed concerns about his hips and legs. His feet pointed toward each other.

As he grew, we realized how bad they had gotten. He would fall on a regular basis. His legs were weak, and he could not walk very far without saying, "Mommy and Daddy, my legs hurt." He couldn't even ride a tricycle. At work one afternoon, I received a phone call from my wife. "Carl, the baby has fallen, and blood's gushing out. I think I see the bone. Please come home now!" I told my boss and went home. We took him to the hospital.

The hospital was extremely busy. I was very glad when he was seen. The doctor stated, "This cut is so deep, I'm going to have to stitch inside and then outside." The wound was almost between his eyes. As the doctor started, the three-year-old started to cry! My wife, pouring out her love as she does so deeply, said, "It will be alright," calling the baby's name. That helped some. But just at that moment, when he was about to cry hard, my wife very softly sang, "Jesus loves me, this I know. For the Bible tells me so. Little ones to Him belong. They are weak, but He is strong." She sang this through the whole procedure. The doctor said, "I have never seen anything like this." Not only was he calm, but he fell asleep.

After healing, we took him back to the doctor to see what we could do to help him with his walking, and he suggested a specialist. The specialist explained that from the womb the leg bones had been twisted. A special brace was needed and would have to work at night on one leg, one leg at a time. It would take several years to straighten each leg. The brace placed pressure on my son's leg and caused him pain. He would cry and kick. It was a parent's worst fear realized: my baby was in pain, and I couldn't help.

After a few years of serving the Lord, we knew God could heal this child. We believed in the power of God. We decided to go to a crusade. My parents watched the other children so my wife, mother-in-law, sister-in-law, and child traveled to Norfolk, Virginia. We arrived.

The morning service was awesome. We felt the presence of the Lord with so many saints praying and singing. The spirit was awesome. We knew God could perform miracles. We prayed and prayed. After awhile, a prayer partner came over and prayed with us. She spoke, "Miracles can happen every day. You must have faith." I put the baby in my lap as I prayed. I thought I felt his bones move inside his legs. I mean I gently moved his feet outward, and I thought they moved straight. Just then, he was wearing a diaper, and he had a blowout. He lost his bowels. It went on my suit, shirt, and my pants. My wife and I took him to the rest room to clean us up. As we walked back, I looked down. His feet and legs looked the same. I was disheartened. I thought, *Had this child been carrying a demon?* I don't know.

My wife took him back to the orthopedic specialist for his usual adjustment a few weeks later. The doctor proceeded to take a series of X-rays. He came to my wife and requested to take a few more X-rays. He said, "Mrs. Wilson, I have taken nine X-rays. Look, here is the old, and here is the new. I will not have to adjust the brace. He won't need it! His legs are straight! As straight as yours or mine." The size of the miracle was apparent. Glory to God!

As summer approached, we bought an above-ground swimming pool and a tricycle with a handle in the back. With the handle in my back, my wife could push to help him. By the end of the summer, the baby was so happy. He would say, "Look, Mommy and Daddy," as he pedaled himself. He would say, "I can do it, I can do it." I give God all the praise for this miracle.

You don't have to know how the miracles happen. Only believe, and have faith that God can perform them. Faith moves mountains. The miracle itself is the evidence!

Is there anything too hard for God to do? Our miracles are only limited to our faith!

Chapter Fourteen

How Serious Is Offending the Holy Ghost?

F irst, let us review some Scriptures.

And when they had prayed, the place was shaken where they were assembled together; and they were all filled with the Holy Ghost, and they spake the word of God with boldness. And the multitude of them that believed were of one heart and of one soul: neither said any of them that ought of the things which he possessed was his own; but they had all things common. And with great power gave the apostles witness of the resurrection of the Lord Jesus: and great grace was upon them all. (Acts 4:31–33)

The Holy Ghost is sent by God. It gives power. Let's get back to the original question. How serious is offending the Holy Ghost?

Neither was there any among them that lacked: for as many as were possessors of lands or houses sold them, and brought the prices of the things that were sold, and laid them down at the apostles' feet: and distribution was made unto every man according as he had need. And Joses, who by the apostles was surnamed Barnabas, (which is, being interpreted, The son of consolation,) a Levite, and of the country of Cyprus, having land, sold it, and brought the money, and laid it at the apostles' feet. (Acts 4:34–37)

They had all agreed to sell and put their possessions together.

But a certain man named Ananias, with Sapphira his wife, sold a possession, and kept back part of the price, his wife also being privy to it, and brought a certain part, and laid it, at the apostles' feet. But Peter said, Ananias, why hath Satan filled thine heart to lie to the Holy Ghost, and to keep back part of the price of the land? Whiles it remained, was it not thine own? and after it was sold, was it not in thine own power? why hast thou conceived this thing in thine heart? thou hast not lied unto men, but unto God. (Acts 5:1–4)

Lying to man is a sin, but they had lied to the Holy Ghost!

And Ananias hearing these words fell down, and gave up the ghost: and great fear came on all them that heard these things. And the young men arose, wound him up, and carried him out, and buried him. And it was about the space of three hours after, when his wife, not knowing what was done, came in. And Peter answered unto her, Tell me whether ye sold the land for so much? And she said, Yea, for so much. Then Peter said unto her, How is it that ye have agreed together to tempt the Spirit of the Lord? behold, the feet of them which have buried thy husband are at the door, and shall carry thee out. Then fell she down straightway at his feet, and yielded up the ghost: and the young men came in, and found her dead, and, carrying her forth, buried her by her husband. And great fear came upon all the church, and upon as many as heard these things. (Acts 5:5–11)

The Holy Ghost is a serious gift with serious consequences. (Consequences mean to accept the results of one's actions.)

CHAPTER FIFTEEN

BLASPHEMY OF THE HOLY GHOST

I s blasphemy of the Holy Ghost the unforgiven sin? And what does that mean?

As I have written earlier, when the Lord Jesus Christ took the sins of the world, past, present and future, upon Himself, we received a tremendous gift—freedom from an eternal hell. We were forgiven from all sins...except one. The Holy Ghost is a gift from God. To deny a gift is an insult, but to mock God's gift is beyond insult.

Blasphemy (From Nelsons Christian Dictionary 2001)

Blasphemy—Insult or mockery of God or His messengers and prophets. Attribution of the works of God to the devil or of the works of the devil to God.

Wherefore I say unto you, All manner of sin and blasphemy shall be forgiven unto men: but the blasphemy against the Holy Ghost shall not be forgiven unto men. And whosoever speaketh a word against the Son of man, it shall be forgiven him: but whosoever speaketh against the Holy Ghost, it shall not be forgiven him, neither in this world, neither in the world to come. (Matthew 12:31–32)

But he that shall blaspheme against the Holy Ghost hath never forgiveness, but is in danger of eternal damnation.
(Mark 3:29)

And whosoever shall speak a word against the Son of man, it shall be forgiven him: but unto him that blasphemeth against the Holy Ghost it shall not be forgiven.
(Luke 12:10)

I want to tell you I have had a lot of thought before I even wrote this chapter or brought this subject up. In this world today, there are so many blinded by Satan that many today think that hell is going to be a party, and to be cool. They will do anything to get in. So telling them a sure thing is a serious thing. Then we must ask ourselves a very important question, Why is blasphemy of the Holy Ghost an unforgivable sin? Did God make a mistake? No! Murder, lying, stealing, and so on are all forgiven. But not blasphemy! God wants you to know!

Why? It's our power. And for the record it's not "The Spirit of God" or "Holy Spirit." It's the Holy Ghost! The Holy Ghost sent by Jesus and God!

Have you ever heard of a deathbed confession? Where someone is about to leave this earth. How important would the last words of a love one be? So then how important were Jesus' last words! After His resurrection, Jesus was here on earth forty days.

And, being assembled together with them, commanded them that they should not depart from Jerusalem, but wait for the promise of the Father, which, saith he, ye have heard of me. For John truly baptized with water; but ye shall be baptized with the Holy Ghost not many days hence. When they therefore were come together, they asked of him, saying, Lord, wilt thou at this time restore again the kingdom to Israel? And he said unto them, It is not for you to know the times or the seasons, which the Father hath put in his own power. But ye shall receive power, after that the Holy Ghost is come upon you: and ye shall be witnesses unto me both in Jerusalem, and in all Judaea, and in Samaria, and unto the uttermost part of the earth. And when he had spoken these things, while they beheld, he was taken up; and a cloud received him out of their sight. (Acts 1:4–9)

When I was baptized, I got it all! Are you saying you are greater than Jesus and the disciples! Our Lord was baptized twice, first to repentance, and then filled with the Holy Ghost!

And when he had said this, he breathed on them, and saith unto them, Receive ye the Holy Ghost. (John 20:22)

Why do so many fall? Simple. They might not have it all.

CHAPTER SIXTEEN

THE MISSION OF THE CHOSEN TWELVE

*These twelve Jesus sent forth, and commanded them, saying,
Go not into the way of the Gentiles, and into any city of the
Samaritans enter ye not.* (Matthew 10:5)

Note: The Jews were the first people Jesus reached out to,
but thanks to their rejection, the Gentiles were later grafted
in.

*But go rather to the lost sheep of the house of Israel. And
as ye go, preach, saying, The kingdom of heaven is at hand.
Heal the sick, cleanse the lepers, raise the dead, cast out
devils: freely ye have received, freely give.* (verses 6–8)

When God gives us spiritual gifts, we are to use them.
When the Holy Ghost rises up in me, I almost immediately
look to pray for someone and lay on hands. The anointing
belongs to God. We don't store it up like canned green beans.
We need God's blessing.

Blessed and holy is he that hath part in the first resurrection: on such the second death hath no power, but they shall be priests of God and of Christ, and shall reign with him a thousand years. (Revelation 20:6)

How can we fight the devil and stay holy? Through the power of the Holy Ghost!

I want to go in the first resurrection.

God's Gift

Two big questions. First, how badly do you want to be used by God? Second, if God gives you the power, will you use it even if it means coming out of your comfort zone? I was working with a produce company, and we were short on drivers.

The owner said, "I need you to take out a truck." I was blessed with an experienced helper. It was a hot summer day, and we were delivering in Ocean City, Maryland. The traffic is unbelievable. It's hard to drive a car, yet alone a twenty-four foot truck. We had made it to our worst stop of the day. We were double parked, blocking traffic, and more trucks trying to come in the same street to deliver.

As I backed up a little bit, I noticed a station wagon go by, and as I was waiting for the helper to come back, I saw the car unload a wheel chair. Then I saw an extremely skinny child who was severely handicapped. I watched his mother struggle to get him into the wheelchair. The Holy Ghost prompted me. I almost leaped out of the truck. There was cash in the truck, and the refer unit was going. I could have been fired. I said, "Ma'am, do you mind if I pray for your child?" We were feet from the boardwalk, and she said yes. I kneeled on one leg, and I prayed, essentially, "Father, we come before You right now. We thank You, Lord, for this day, and we humbly ask you to strengthen this young man. Give his body a restoration, a renewing if it is Your will. And strengthen his family. In Jesus' name, amen." I said, "Thank you, ma'am!" then proceeded back to the truck. About one minute later, the helper came back.

The Holy Ghost power that was flowing through me was so strong it's hard to describe. The helper said, "Hey, you could have gone on to the next stop. I would have caught up to you." I said, "That's okay. I had something very special to do." He just looked puzzled. Did the young man gain more strength? I may never know. The whole point is, Can God count on you to be used for His glory and not your own? Think of the people all over the world. Some are starving, some in prisons for no reason, babies crying for love, sick people all over the world. Does this bother you? It's only getting worse, and what about their souls, which will burn forever? It's bad enough their life here was not so pleasant, but they face eternal prison! Who will help? Who will stand? Who will lead? Will you be one? God wants to use many, but they will not heed the call! And many leaders even refuse the power before them. Time is getting short. Will you be a part of the last day's crusade? With God's Holy Ghost anointing, you will stand! Pray, ask, seek, and knock. The Lord Jesus loves you. He needs you. Souls are in the balance.

CHAPTER SEVENTEEN

THE POWER OF THE HOLY GHOST

How powerful is the Holy Ghost? How powerful is God? I don't think the human mind can comprehend God's level of intelligence or His unlimited power! Why do we not use the power God has given us? The God we take for granted, that holds our next breath, that has showed us signs and wonders, healings, deliverance, and miracles, also wants us to believe and use the power source He has put in place, the Holy Ghost!

Here is an example of the Holy Ghost in action! My son was hot with fever. They stated a flu virus was going around. My wife, concerned, had given the child over-the-counter fever reducer. He was in a seesaw—fever up, fever down. The second evening, his fever reached 103.2! A call to our pediatrician had informed us there was not much they could do. Fluid, rest, fever reducers. His fever had clearly gotten my attention! So I decided I was going to get God's attention! I proceeded to our family room that doubled for our sanctuary. I found my knees and prayer. I felt strong anointing; the presence of the Holy

Ghost was strong. I made my way to the bedside of my son. I placed my hands on his head, I prayed, the fever departed almost immediately. My son recovered quickly. Glory to God!

Releasing the Power

After receiving the gift of the Holy Ghost, I was sure God was going to get upset with me. Why? Well, as with Samson, God can pull your anointing at any time at His discretion. So every few hours, after receiving the Holy Ghost, I would say, "Holy Ghost, are you still with me?" My spirit would quicken, letting me know He was still with me! A new question now surfaces, why did God give me the gift? And when was He going to release the power? Well, it didn't take long to answer that question! My wife and I decided to go and see a well-known teacher and pastor. You probably know him. My mother-in-law and sister-in-law were present.

This event, which about nine hundred people attended each evening, was power-packed. First, there would be praise and worship, then preaching, teaching, then an altar call for those seeking more from God. Our first two nights were educational but mostly uneventful. Not that I'm a little child that has to be entertained. What I'm saying is having the Holy Ghost power fill the house! Still night after night I expected a miracle. In anticipation, we arrived early to get good seats. This evening, the guest speaker was about two rows in front of us. I could actually see the anointing on him, almost like a shimmer on his shoulders. His message that evening was powerful. At the end his altar call was for anyone seeking the Holy Ghost to come forward for prayer. And I want all ministers who are willing to come pray for these. Also anyone led to pray for these, come forward. I felt a natural pulling to go up front. I could not resist. My wife and sister-in-law made their way up front so I went to pray for them first. I was about to get a surprise. The Holy Ghost was about to make His presence known in a mighty way. I don't remember the exact order. It was amazing. As I placed my hands gently on my wife's face, she received a gift of anointing. Let me get this straight: I give nothing. God is the giver. We are just the vessel the power goes through. When I prayed for another, something was broken off. I was speaking in tongues, praising God. I was led to go down the line. I did not force myself on anyone. I was led and asked a lady, "Do you want me to pray for you?" She said, "I'm a Catholic. I've never heard of this before!" I said, "Ma'am, this is real! God's power is real!" I told her when God laid me out on the floor and filled me with the Holy Ghost, he changed my eye color from brown to green! She said she was okay with it. I prayed for her, and the anointing fell. What she felt, I don't know. But I do know this. She had the biggest smile on her face as I walked away. For the record, I tell the truth in everything. This lady could have been of any branch of faith. I do not discriminate.

At this point, I made my way to my mother-in-law. She seems to be in a constant health battle. The push to the front was great. I could only reach for her from behind some chairs. I came up and placed my hand gently on her head. As I started to pray, bam (well, I could not think of another word), down she went right on the concrete floor. It just so happened that my wife and sister-in-law were returning to their seats. They saw their mother hit the floor! They cried Mama. My wife said, "Carl, Mama." I was under such anointing all I could do was speak in tongues and praise God. I went back into the crowd. I asked a man, "Do you want me to pray for you?" Yes. I prayed for him, and bam, he fell back into some chairs! Then a lady standing nearby said, "Please pray for me!" I went and prayed for her. The anointing hit her, and she was all smiles! Then I asked another man if I could pray for him. He reluctantly said yes. I was on fire! But this encounter was different. He could not feel anything. I could not understand why. First, I have learned not to try to figure out God! Second, some profess they want to change and want more from God, but deep down inside they have absolutely no plans of changing. Then some want to change so bad they are willing to do almost anything...except get out of their seat! The devil has them, as if they were glued in their seats! The facts are this, God's power is real and a gift for those who really want to submit. The power is real! It's simple. God commands we submit, then He blesses. No submission, no blessing.

On the way home, we were all so happy! I had so much anointing still in me. I said, "What I need to do is go home and pray over our cat!" We all knew I was kidding, but God can change even the animals. God's power and blessings are incredible. Glory to God !

The Gift!

God the Father, Giver of Life

Gave us our Life!

Gave His only begotten Son for our salvation!

He gave His life!

He, Jesus—God, gave us another comforter, the Holy Ghost!

This Gift is from God!

This Gift brings power and spiritual gifts!

God is the giver of gifts.

He gives…gives…gives!

Let's not insult the gift or the giver!

HOLY GHOST FACTS

He is not for sale and cannot be bought. (Acts 8:18)

He gives power to serve, real power, not for self-indulgence. (Acts 1:8)

It is not yours! It belongs to God to give or take at His will. (John 14:26)

May increase or decrease at God's will. (Romans 5:13)

A gift from God. (Acts 2:33)

Will not dwell in a dirty vessel, an unclean temple. He requires that you be sin free. (Acts 2:38)

Still available, a gift from God to those who obey! (Acts 5:32)

In the Bible ninety times for a reason!

Jesus' final words before being translated to heaven! (Acts 1:5, 8)

Some died for lying to the Holy Ghost! (Acts 9:17)

Blasphemy, the only unforgiven sin. (Luke 12:10, 12)

The gift is not given at salvation unless ordered by God!

Some of the many evidences of the gift are speaking in tongues, prophesy, healings. (2 Peter 1:21)

The Godhead has never changed! God the Father, God the Son, and God the Holy Ghost!

No Holy Ghost means no Jesus. (Luke 1:35)

People still resist. (Acts 7:51)

Was given to certain disciples by breathing on them. (John 20:22)

Was given by the laying on of hands. (Acts 8:17)

Some received the Holy Ghost, then were baptized. (Acts 10:47)

Available to all, even the Gentiles. (Acts 10:45)

We are ordered by Jesus, Go, teach, and baptize in Holy Ghost. (Matthew 28:19)

The Comforter. (John 14:26)

The Holy Ghost bears record in heaven. (1 John 5:7)

When Jesus died on the cross, He gave up the ghost!

I expressed from the very beginning of the book that you should study the truth for yourself. Don't just take my word on it! Scriptural facts speak for themselves.

For those who claim the Holy Spirit and Holy Ghost are the same,

And whosoever shall speak a word against the Son of man, it shall be forgiven him: but unto him that blasphemeth against the Holy Ghost it shall not be forgiven.

(Luke 12:10)

Plain enough!

CLOSING

O ur very Christian faith is under attack!

It comes from many sources. Our main attack comes from our own lack of power. Sure there are plenty of messages about power. It's like talking about pizza. You know, dripping with fresh hot cheese, fresh baked crust, hand tossed and finished in a brick oven. Super large slice loaded with toppings, garden fresh vegetables, and home-made sauce with fresh garlic and basil, lightly sprinkled with oregano and grated fresh aged parmesan cheese, so hot that you have to be careful not to burn your mouth. There's only one catch: you have to ask for it. It's the same with the Holy Ghost. There are many big talkers about power, but few real seekers for the Holy Ghost! We have within our reach the ability to change the world for God. God wants us to use this power. So many today are blinded by false doctrine or lack of knowledge. Some will stick their heads in the sand. How far as Christians do we allow the world and Satan to try to dictate who we are and what we stand for? When are we as a body going to unite and realize the truth is the truth?

Christ's last words were about the Holy Ghost, and it is the only unpardonable sin! Our power to stand where demons tremble and chains of bondage are broken, God's power is unlimited! Let's rise to the level of our commitment, and release the promise, the gift, the comforter; the Holy Ghost!

God bless you!

Minister Carl L. Wilson, Jr.

For prayer, correspondence, speaking engagements, or book tour information, contact Minister Carl L. Wilson, Jr., at prayerunderGod@aol.com.

This book did not mean to offend anyone or group. It was written with love.